Green
Side
UP

Wes R. Porter

Green
Side
UP

Growing a Perfect Lawn in Northern Climates

Fitzhenry & Whiteside

To my wife who, after over a quarter-century,
still laughs at my jokes.

Fitzhenry and Whiteside Limited
195 Allstate Parkway
Markham, Ontario L3R 4T8

In the United States:
311 Washington Street
Brighton, Massachusetts 02135

www.fitzhenry.ca   godwit@fitzhenry.ca

Fitzhenry & Whiteside acknowledges with thanks Canada Council for the Arts, and the
Ontario Arts Council for their support of our publishing program. We acknowledge the
financial support of the Government of Canada through the Book Publishing Industry
Development Program (BPIDP) for our publishing activities.

Canadian Cataloguing in Publication Data

Porter, Wes
Green side up: growing the perfect lawn in northern climates

Rev. ed.
ISBN 1-55041-382-1

1. Lawns – Canada. I Title.

SB433.P67 1999   635.9'647'0971   C98-931743-9

The Publisher would like to thank the following for graciously supplying pictures for *Green Side Up.*

Line drawings on pages 3, 4, 6, 11, 18, 46 and 53 are from *The Illustrated History of Gardening* (Lyon's Press, 1998), reprinted
  with permission from Tony Lyons
Original sketches on pages 14, 16 and 86 were provided by Peter Mikos
Pictures on pages 27 and 34 are reprinted with kind permission from The T. Eaton Company Limited
Pictures on pages 29, 31, 51, 89, 92, 97 are reprinted with permission from The Toro Company
Photographs on pages 35, 43, 47, 94 are from Lee Valley Tools Mid-Summer 1998 Catalogue, reprinted with permission
  from Lee Valley Tools
Drawings on pages 60, 61, 104, 107, 108, 109, 111, 117 and 120 are from *1997 White Rose/W. H. Perron Yard & Garden
4th Anniversary Edition Catalogue*, reprinted with permission from White Rose
Photograph of Derek Green's garden ornamentation on page 127 provided by Patricia Easton

Every effort has been made to locate copyright holders.
The publisher will welcome any information that will allow it to correct any errors or omissions.

Design: Kerry Designs
Printed in Canada

Table of Contents

Introduction

God Almighty planted the first garden and indeed it is the purest of human pleasures. It is the greatest refreshment to the spirit of man; without which buildings and places are but gross handiwork.   Sir Francis Bacon Lord Chancellor (1625)

Twelve years of grassroots gardening have passed since *Green Side Up* first made its appearance. Mr. Robert Fitzhenry, president of Fitzhenry and Whiteside, had requested I write the book while I was assisting him in making the grass surrounding his new publishing headquarters look like something resembling a lawn and less like an unsuccessful agricultural experiment.

There is good reason for a second, vastly revised edition. The grass has grown long and lush over the past dozen years. Massive changes have taken place in the world of gardening, now the acknowledged leisure time activity of eighty percent of the population. Imagine, twelve years ago we were still calling gardening a hobby. Gardening is now a $4 billion a year business, second only to wheat in agricultural yield for Canada. The world spice and herb trade, by comparison, is less than half this amount. And in this period of exploding consumer enthusiasm for gardening, the federal government has cut back funding of ornamental plant programmes and is doing its best to destroy the Dominion Arboretum in Ottawa, one of the world's most respected collections.

Most books on lawns are of little assistance to us in the northern climes. We are not the same as our cousins south o' the border down Washington way, nor do our climates and soils compare to those of that weird, wonderful little island archipelago anchored off the northwest coast of Europe. Our equipment for lawn care may look pretty much the same, but much else, fertilizers, insecticides, fungicides and herbicides, is not. We also use, thanks to the decisiveness of our elected leaders, not just one but two different systems of measurement. Give a politician an inch and she thinks she's a ruler.

Our climate is different. You can fly out of Toronto in a blizzard and be walking a few hours later through Vancouver's Stanley Park in your shirtsleeves. And in order to do so, you must endure the displays of rhododendrons and other exotics immediately outside Vancouver Airport. This is how British Columbia gets even with eastern gardeners. Its mild and moist coastal climate causes lawns to flourish as nowhere else in Canada. Then again, Canadians elsewhere miss the opportunity of finding a sasquatch gamboling on the grass.

Gardening is popular because it is one of the last refuges where individual expression is possible. One anonymous sage summed it up best: "gardening is the mirror of the mind." This may explain our political gardens as well. What method you use when gardening is entirely of your own choice. This book might be likened to the guide on a trekking vacation. It indicates the way, but does not presume to insist that the author's personal beliefs be followed. If something works for you and gives you pleasure, do it, and let the experts join that great compost heap in the sky.

This book is like hitting a smiling astrologist: it attempts to strike a happy medium. While admitting that chemicals and mechanization cannot solve any and every gardening problem, the rigid rejection of such does not either.

Another compromise is to admit that a lawn is not always the answer. There are, as the horticultural industry is pleased to call them, alternate ground covers. Very small urban front yards, heavily wooded back gardens, steep slopes, and vacation homes are possible candidates for this treatment. I explore ground covers, including charts, and even plants, in a separate chapter. There is also a separate chapter on those newly re-discovered sensations, ornamental grasses.

Happiness, Sir Harry Lauder reminded us once, is one of the few things in the world which doubles every time you share it. Gardening often seems to lead to the achievement of a ripe old age. It seems only reasonable then to graft these two together.

And, finally, why "green side up?"

Urban legend has it that a landscape contractor was talking with his client. Every few minutes during the conversation, he would excuse himself, go to the window, fling it open and bellow, "green side up!" Finally his customer could stand it no longer. "Why," she queried, "do you keep going to the window and shouting 'green side up?'" The contractor explained "I've got a crew out there laying your sod and, man, are they ever stupid!"

Wes R.Porter
Toronto,1999

Background to Lawns and Gardens

A sweep of lawn surrounded with suitable shrubs and flowers separated from it by walks of beautiful gravel.   William Cobbett, English nurseryman, journalist, writer (1828)

The *Oxford English Dictionary* informs us in its third definition that a lawn is "an area of grass-covered ground which is kept mown and smooth in a garden, park, etc." It can also be a form of linen or fine cotton fabric used nowadays for part of a bishop's ecclesiastical clothing (which word is derived from the French city of Laon). Still, on the authority of the *OED*, it would seem that lawn, the modern word, comes from the ancient, and now archaic laund, meaning a glade or open space in woods, particularly in the New Forest of west Hampshire, England.

Lawns are the carpets of the garden. They set every other part of the landscape off to perfection. Most carpets are not noticed unless they become old, threadbare, and tattered. And so it is with lawns. For at least a millennium, humans have strived to ensure only the best grasses were selected and kept trimmed, with or without additional intruding plants, according to the fashionable dictates of the day.

The average homeowner has often been battered by the strident vocalisms of the politically correct. Lawns have become a popular topic. Lawns, our politically correct brethren claim, are not natural. On the contrary, most reliable sociographic sources suggest that we humans did not even haul ourselves up onto our hind legs until we came down from the trees and out onto the grassy plains of East Africa. We are what we are today because we developed on those grassland plains.

Lawns are wasteful is another argument held forth. Actually, lawns reduce or prevent erosion, reduce both particulate and gaseous pollution, lower temperatures, and act, especially in rural areas, as efficient fire breaks from surrounding inflammable vegetation and crops. Lawns waste neither water nor nutrients. Given these

benefits, it is hard to see why anyone would begrudge them such support. Incidentally, independent scientifically-conducted research by recognized authorities has shown that water percolating through lawns emerges cleaner than that supplied by many North American municipal authorities.

It has been claimed that the modern lawn was invented by noted American landscape architect, Frederick Law Olmstead (1822-1903), who first rose to prominence when his design for the competition to laying out Central Park, New York beat out over thirty-two competitors. A few years later in 1868, Olmstead received a commission to design the Chicago suburb of Riverside, one of the first planned communities. He demanded that each house be set back from the street ten metres (thirty feet) and forbade intervening walls. This created a sylvan look, a favorite motif of the architect, and gave the not unworthy impression of one community living together in a park.

Why Olmstead's efforts entered modern mythology as the first lawns is puzzling. Modest examination indicates that lawns were recognized as contributions to the community as far back as the Dark Ages (said to have been called such because there were so many knights). During that time, the nobility resided in castles around which it was thought advisable to maintain a belt of cleared land lest some enemy creep up and surprise the household – unarmoured and unarmed. A "mount" or artificial hill as a look-out post provided additional insurance against surprise attacks. In time, life became somewhat safer (than living in a

New Brunswick Ghost Kills Grass?

According to Stuart Trueman's, Ghosts, Pirates and Treasure Trove *(1975), Patricia Jenkin's house in Gagetown, New Brunswick is said to be haunted by a female ghost. A short distance from the front door is a large oval track of dead grass which looks as if someone regularly walks on it. The area has been excavated, fresh soil brought in and grass seed sown, but still nothing will grow. Miss Jenkin has suggested the oval is where the ghost takes her exercise.*

modern North American city) and the mount, which had been kept covered with grass to prevent erosion while offering a clear view, became a meeting place, with turf benches to sit on for the gentry.

One of the first recorded description of lawns comes from the pen of theologian, Hugh of St. Victor, who wrote of a walled garden in the early 1100s, presumed to have been in France. It not only had trees and flowers, but was improved and made delightful with green grass. In 1240, the Englishman Bartholomew de Glanville described a pleasure garden centred on a fountain surrounded by grass. That idea was expanded two decades later by Albertus Magnus, who not only recommended the addition of turf benches, but gave sensible cultural instructions for establishing a lawn by removing weeds, levelling the area, and covering it with luxurious sod – although Magnus believed sod was best beaten level with wooden mallets.

De Glanville, notwithstanding, it appears (from surviving records) that the English lacked not only lawns, but also advanced ornamental horticulture, until at least the late Tudor times. France was the place to be, or possibly northern Italy. In the blooming town of Bologna, one Pietro de'Crescenzi advised on landscaping in 1305 using the by then well-established idea of turf seats. In an illustrated edition of his work a century and a half later, a primitive landscape contractor is shown pounding the sod to form lawn. By the fifteenth century, the French were also adept not only at creating gardens, but also at painting them. One painting by Renaud de Montalbahn depicts a couple seated on a lawn, leaning against brick-sided turf seats, a greyhound-like dog beside them, a nearby fountain gushing water, and two planters, one filled with flowers, the other with early proof of a tasteless topiary. Perhaps the latter is cause for the troubled expression on the couple's faces.

Another French illustration shows a walled garden with a youth and his instructor standing outside. A woman with a large key and a suspicious look on her face stands in the doorway giving access to the garden. Above her head is a sign proclaiming "Nature." We can see three young ladies inside the garden strolling over lawns surrounded by flower-bedecked beds. Labels inform us that these maidens represent Pallas, Goddess of Wisdom, Juno, the Queen of the Gods (virtue herself), and Venus who, as Goddess of Love, stands naked below a shady tree. The youth outside the garden is meant to make the proper choice as to the life he will live. Lawns, as the carpets of life's garden, show off everything in it to best effect.

The Emperor Babur (c. 1482-1530) or, to give him his proper name, Zahir-ed-din Mohammed, a direct descendant of the famed and feared Tamerlane (conqueror of most of India and founder

Man Eats Grass

According to the London Times *(May 2, 1940), a British gentleman named Branson treated himself regularly to a healthy diet of mowings from the Mitcham Common gold greens. Preparation included washing the greens well before mixing them with lettuce, rose petals, oats, sugar, currants and sultanas. Mr. Branson's ultimate fate is unknown.*

Is sod always laid over fifteen centimetres (six inches) of good, rich top soil? Not according to one of the largest American grass seed and fertilizer suppliers. One of Scott's research headquarters buildings in Marysville, Ohio, a short distance from Columbus, has an enormous lawn laid on a base of solid concrete. The lawn has flourished for many years nurtured with generous levels of water and fertilizer.

of its Mogul dynasty), was a superb poet and landscaper who left gardens in Persia, Afghanistan, northern India and Kashmir. His autobiography records that he directed lawns to be installed as well. By 1519 Babur was rapsodizing over the beauty of the landscape at the Bagh i-Wafa, or Garden of Fidelity, near Jelalabad. He particularly admired the clover mix of the lawn.

One of the earliest illustrations we have of English lawns comes not from a painting but from tapestries still in existence at Montacute House, Somerset. In this instance, a garden inspired the embroidery, although in future years the reverse would be true. Needlework patterns suggest new and different designs to gardens, culminating in the works of Le Notre two centuries later. The Montacute Tapestries depict small lawns edged with flower beds containing what are apparently garden pinks or hardy carnations as well as tulips, Madonna lilies, and fruit trees, along with ornamental ponds. These works date from the fifteenth century and seem to have been surprisingly advanced by modern standards, particularly when compared with existing French

and Italian paintings of approximately the same date.

Although Elizabeth I and her court were reputedly fans of tennis played on grass courts, let us not forget the Scottish contribution to lawn development through the inventions of golf and lawn bowling.

Which leads us to an interesting problem: who cut the grass and how was it cut? The Scots used what might be termed lawn-moo-ers. Cows kept the rougher lawns fairly well trimmed, but, because no wandering Australian with his didgeridu had yet introduced the frisbee – organic or otherwise – to utilize cow flaps, those deposits made it imperative to find something which trimmed the grass closely but left a neater aftermath. Sheep and goats found favour with the American armed forces because of their ability to keep grass trimmed around munitions dumps. Human operators and gas-driven mechanized mowers are apparently too much of a danger and grass is a superb ground cover around such areas. In earlier days, humans with sickles and scythes were relied upon to produce perfect cuts. English garden writer, John Claudius Loudon, writing around 1825, recorded that when three labourers used scythes, the trimmed grass posed a problem. They would be followed by a man with a hay rake. He, in turn, was followed by a woman or boy with a four-foot besom (or birch broom of the kind commonly depicted as propulsion units for witches). Finally, last in line would come a man with a horse and cart, and a boy with a pair of boards to remove the piles left by the other labourers.

In the seventeenth century, Andre Mollet recorded that sheep were encouraged to graze grass wherever a high-quality sod was to be lifted. Mollet noted that the work must be done after early September, or weeds would result. Sod laid in the fall was first compacted with a wooden roller, then with a stone roller. It would be scythed twice a week in order to grow dense and lush. Modern gardeners may blanch at the thought of using sickles or scythes, but it is truly amazing how closely, and neatly, experienced labourers can trim a lawn with these ancient tools. Parks in many of the world's developing nations are trimmed by men wielding "bush knives" – curved blades just under fifty centimetres (two feet) long, cold-hammered out of scrap steel and sharpened on a suitable rock.

The American Revolution, notwithstanding, inhabitants south of the border still admired much that was English. When Thomas Jefferson laid out Monticello, his Paladian villa in Virginia, he used sweeping lawns between groups of native

The Dogs of Paris

- *a quarter-million dogs reside in Paris, France*
- *they deposit an average of 25 tons of excrement each and every day*
- *70 specially-designed vehicles, officially known as "caninettes," are used to clean up the mess*
- *these machines, a cross between a vacuum and a motorized scooter, cost $11.5 US million annually*
- *despite this attention to detail, 50% of the excrement is missed, causing 650 human hospitalizations a year*

American and exotic imported trees. Many other well-to-do, newly-minted Americans visited England to admire the verdure of Shakespeare's scepter'd isle, and to bring back the new-fangled landscaping and lawn ideas. Napoleon's Empress Josephine employed her jardin anglais at the estate of Mailmaison much to her husband's annoyance. She also had lawn bowling, perhaps it was because a Scottish gardener first introduced such landscaping to France. Josephine, who left so much to modern gardeners with roses and other collections at Mailmaison, would be divorced and banished from her home and garden by her husband, but she did return to Mailmaison to die.

In Canada, or at least in those areas settled for some time, lawns were trimmed by sheep and cattle – at least until the indigenous Canada geese discovered the succulent feast.

Canadian geese keep grass short. Unfortunately, geese also generate large quantities of guano when feasting on lawns. The two do not harmonize well, and guano does not improve access on surrounding paths.

Thus emerges a situation made-to-measure for any inventor and/or entrepreneur. Such a man was the English engineer, Edward Beard Budding (c. 1796-1846). Budding was employed in a textile factory which required the raised pile on some fabrics to be neatly trimmed. This was accomplished by a spiral-bladed device. Budding incorporated this trimming device into a machine suitable for treating lawns. The resultant lawn cutter made a fearsome clatter, and Budding dared only try it out after dark. The machine worked. Budding patented his design in 1830 and commenced manufacturing the following year.

Some English landowners began to notice that their labourers actually enjoyed pushing and pulling those early, somewhat unwieldy, lawn mowers, although horses with special boots on their hooves were required in some cases to facilitate the work. As time passed, landowners were offered several new and novel mowers, including a tricycle-propelled model and an adapted steamroller. Many employers were tempted to try the lawn mowing task themselves.

It was an American, of course, who brought us the joys of peaceful early weekend mornings broken by the noise from roaring, exhaust-belching motorized mowers. Former U.S. Army Colonel, Edwin George, formed a company in Detroit following World War I to manufacture and retail his newly-invented "Moto-Mower." Apparently George made the prototype by utilizing the gasoline engine which powered his wife's washing machine. Whether his wife ever got her motor back, history does not record.

A half-century later, the *Saturday Evening Post*

Victorian Language of Flowers

Forbidden by society to work, middle-class young ladies in Victorian England amused themselves by inventing messages concealed in drawings of flowers and other portions of plants. Each flower stood for a separate word, sentiment, or phrase. According to this code, grass stood for "utility."

claimed there were twenty-five million home lawns covering five million acres in the United States. In California – where else? – lawn owners placed clear bottles filled with water on their front lawn since, according to one professor's "urban mythology," this was an infallible way to discourage dogs. One enterprising and skeptical observer reported that at least one passing pooch treated the lawn bottle as only a dog can. This did nothing to stop the legend from passing over the Pacific to, of all places, New Zealand. In Wisconsin, a clear bottle filled with water and placed on the front lawn was reported to discourage rabbits. And one Australian, of whom Edward Beard Budding would have been proud, invented a rabbit powered mower – a cylindrical wire cage which rolled across the lawn while a pair of rabbits inside nibbled at the grass.

The rotary mower arrived on the scene in 1949 and was first used to maintain rougher grass, such as that found in orchards. By 1955, the British government had decided to remove the mandatory driving licenses necessary for operating mowers. A decade later, inventive New York police used unmarked lawn mowers left along the roadside to conceal their then primitive radar traps. In Norway, a man has been charged with operating a motor mower while under the influence.

Lawns seem to have been very attractive to earlier settlers and cartographers of Canada. The town of Lawn, adjacent to Newfoundland's Notre Dame Bay at 46.57N, 55.32W, stands as might be expected on Lawn Bay, which is guarded by the cape, Lawn Head. Lawn, in Pontiac County, Quebec, may have separatists seething but they should look back to the opening sentences of this chapter. British Columbia has not one but two Lawn Points, one in Rupert, the other across the water in the Queen Charlotte Islands, where also exists the unincorporated Lawnhill at 53.25N, 131.55W.

For the record, there is also a homestead in Queensland, Australia called Lawnhill, while Lawn is the name of a farm in South Africa, and in Taylor County, Texas, south of Abilene, lies the town of Lawn, population 79,530.

England, which had done so much to encourage the landscaped use of lawns, uses the name for its farms: two in each of the counties of Derbyshire, Staffordshire and Wiltshire and a single representation in Buckinghamshire, Cambridgeshire, Dorset, Hampshire, Leicestershire, and North Yorkshire. Wales has a Lawn Farm in Powys, and the British managed to

Canadians Love Lawns

- *60% of Canadians derive satisfaction from knowing their lawns have no weeds*
- *73% of Canadians say that it is important to have a well-groomed lawn*
- *53% of respondents admitted that they prefer Sunday afternoons relaxing in their gardens to visiting their in-laws.*
- *two-thirds of Canadians spend an average of 3.3 hours a week caring for their lawns: more time than they spend walking the dog, swimming or sun-tanning*
- *residents of the Atlantic region and of smaller towns prefer lawn care to cooking*

produce the movie, "The Lawnmower Man," based on a novel by Stephen King. And don't forget "Keep Off the Grass," a 1937 Broadway production with Jackie Gleason, Jimmy Durante, Larry Adler and Ray Bolger.

All of which goes to prove that, critics notwithstanding, grass and lawns have been around for over a thousand years as an essential component of landscaping, of advanced civilization, and of ordinary, normal, everyday life. It is with reluctance that we depart from these fascinating facts to examine what you have been waiting impatiently for – how to grow the perfect lawn in northern climates.

Under the sod,
Under the trees,
Lies the body
Of Jonathan Pease.
He is not here,
But only his pod,
He has shelled his peas
And gone to God.

epitaph on a tombstone in the Old North Cemetery, Nantucket

Grass Species

Grass is the forgiveness of nature – her constant benediction. Forests decay, harvests perish, flowers vanish, but grass is immortal.   Brian Ingalls

Grass is grass, right? Wrong! All grasses may appear the same from eye level, but a worm's eye view quickly shows us that this is anything but so. Botanically-true grasses are from the family, Gramineae. Human nature being what it is, many other plants are known as "grasses" when they are anything but: "sweet grass," for example, is not a true grass. Bamboo, however, is a giant grass although even the contemplation of mowing a hundred-foot high lawn is, as Winston Churchill was wont to say, off-putting.

There are over thirty grass species common to Canada, although like most of our human population, few are natives. Some are extremely durable and desirable lawn grasses, Kentucky bluegrass *(Poa pratensis)*, for example. Many more are highly obnoxious weeds. The notorious crab grass *(Digitaria ischaeum)* and barnyard grass *(Echinochloa crusgalli)* are far too well known. Many of these undesirable grasses originated in Europe and Asia, "Eurasia." Only a half dozen or so of the thirty-plus grasses growing here in Canada are suitable for home lawns, and no one species will perform optimally under all conditions likely to be found in any one area of the country.

We live in what the climatologists cheerfully call the Temperate Zone, where specific regions experience blizzards and/or torrential rains or drought, and temperatures range from the near tropic to amongst the lowest ever recorded on this planet. Because of these extremes, as well as the limitations of each grass, Canadians have developed and combined two solutions for grass cultivation.

The first is to select and breed preferred strains of different grasses to achieve cultivated varieties or, as the horticultural crowd calls them nowadays, cultivars. Cultivars are often preferred over a simple original variety, although natural crosses do, of course, occur in the wild. These hybrid grasses have such desirable characteristics as resistance to drought and some pathogens, and toleration of shade, heavy foot traffic and the like. Although cultivars do not perform well under all circumstances – advertising claims notwithstanding – they are a distinct improvement over individual species.

The second cultivation solution combines both cultivars and species into homogeneous mixtures, much in the manner that sand, lime, gravel and other ingredients, when combined in the proper ration, become immensely strong concrete. Lawn seed mixtures rarely consist of a solitary species – improved Kentucky bluegrass *(Poa pratensis)*, for example. They usually include as well:

- red fescue *(Festuca rubra)* which withstands shaded, cool conditions
- chewing fescue *(F.r. commutata)* which tolerates drought
- tall fescue *(F. elatior)*, suitable for shaded, cool conditions
- Italian ryegrass *(Lolium multiflorum)* which germinates quickly and assists by protecting slower species
- perennial ryegrass *(L. perenne)* which withstands heavy foot traffic

Let us have a closer look at the characteristics of each component before plunking down our hard-earned dollars for something which, if Brian Ingalls is to be believed, is immortal. Time to meet your mats.

Sod Farms

One of my favourite stories features two yuppies watching a huge tractor trailer loaded with sod manoeuvre down their urban street. "It must be wonderful," sighs one to the other, "to be able to send out your lawn to be mown." If the truth be told, most homeowners, as well as most commercial business seeking a new lawn choose sod over seed. While not "instant grass," sod involves less work than seed once the sowing is completed, and it can be walked over within a few days of installation. You do need to know, however, how reliable the companies in the business of producing sod are.

Growing sod calls for a heavy initial financial investment, plus expert and careful maintenance. Turf farms generally only grow the best cultivar blends for the areas they supply. Better yet, sod farms are generally located in the same geographic areas so the grasses are already acclimatized to local conditions. A sod farm usually limits itself to a very select number of blends – sometimes just two: one for sun, the other for shade.

Consumers who desire instant coverage, who can afford the price, and are who willing to settle for nothing less than complete perfection will be delighted with sod delivered directly from the local sod farm by the company's own trucks. Sod is usually sold by the yard (metric-enhanced bureaucrats notwithstanding) and "yard" is turf terminol-

---

Groucho Marx a Lawn Jockey

Groucho claimed that once, when he was mowing his lawn in Hollywood dressed in very casual clothing, sans his famous but false upper lip adornment, a woman driving an expensive car stopped close by.
"How much do you get paid for doing this?" she demanded
"Nothing, but the lady who lives here lets me sleep with her," Groucho shot back.

ogy for a square yard. Confusing the matter further, a yard of sod is not a square but a strip, six feet long, eighteen inches wide. Rolled up, it weighs about thirty pounds. If the weather is wet and the sod has become soaked, the weight increases to at least seventy pounds for the first five rolls lifted, and apparently increases rapidly for the remainder of the load.

When ordering sod, do not worry about the number of rolls you require. Telephone or fax your order to the sod farm of your choice. State the measurements of the area you wish converted into a lawn. The sod farm's sales representative will convert your measurements into the proper amount of rolls required. You can rely on this as an accurate calculation with no attempt to "oversell." Given the quantities of sod each and every farm deals with every day of the season, together with the industry's overall reputation for integrity, sod farms are unlikely to cheat you for the sake of making a sale of a few extra rolls. Like reputable garden centres, most farms belong to the same provincial trade associations as lawn centres do, and are proud to display this information on advertisements, literature and invoices.

The Ryegrasses (Lolium spp.)

This grass is not that to which the Scotsman sang of when inquiring if he should kiss, "coming through the rye." Nor does it have anything to do with the world famous beverage, rye whiskey. Ryegrasses are based on the extremely hardy cereal used today to make rye bread, and which, a century or so ago, was a common source of ergot poisoning for poor European peasants.

The *Lolium* species are often known outside the ornamental horticultural context as "darnel." Ryegrass is an alien, short-lived perennial, with rather wiry stems, and is important agriculturally as a pasture grass. It has escaped to populate roadsides and vacant land where it may grow as high as sixty centimetres (two feet). The ryegrass stalk is wavy and not straight, with the seeds alternating on either side.

Ryegrasses are fast germinators and make good "nurse grass" assistants for other more desirable species in lawns. They have also found favour in land reclamations and similar constructions because they establish themselves quickly and prevent erosion. Given their tough, wiry nature, ryegrasses also find much use in sports fields and playgrounds, but because they are not soft, and are poor at absorbing falls, they are usually blended with more desirable selections. Ryegrass tolerates shade better than Kentucky bluegrass cultivars, but not as well as the fescues.

A small percentage of perennial ryegrass, *L. perenne*, should be included in most quality lawn seed blends. Notice that the word "perennial" is emphasized. Some cheap blends may use an annual ryegrass seed. Such practices should best be met only with rye looks. If for some reason, an entire lawn of perennial ryegrass is desired, it should be sown at two kilograms per hundred square metres (four and one-half pounds per one hundred and twenty square yards).

Creeping Bent Grass *(Agrostis palustris)*

Whenever anyone contemplates owning a lawn "like a putting green" or "a bowling green," creeping bent grass is the grass species they need. Usually, however, after prospective lawn owners discover all the facts about this species, its alternatives seem more attractive.

Bent grasses must be kept mowed so extremely low that only reel lawn mowers can be used. If the lawn area is large, the cost of a powered reel mower will be found equally so. The grass must be mowed about every three days. And since the cut is so low, any injury or imperfection shows up as obviously as a dandelion on more conventional lawns. Bent grass requires very high levels of fertilizer and water, especially the latter, as it is quite intolerant of drought.

Whatever the weather or general climatic conditions, bent grasses are highly susceptible to every disease known to the Gramineae, and then some. Given the cost of lawn fungicides, and discounting the obvious dangers of pollution, the bent grass lawn option will most probably be rejected, at least by the home gardener. Greens keepers, on the other hand, take enormous pride in their immaculate bent grass playing surfaces. Greens keepers are also paid exceptionally well, and command considerable budgets to produce their artwork.

The Fescues *(Festuca spp.)*

A very useful group of grasses, the fescues are by far the best choice for shaded areas, where they compete well with tree roots for moisture and nutrients. All fescues tolerate dry conditions well. Their fertilizer requirements are modest and they stay in good shape. However, because fescues are used to growing in cool shade, they do not thrive in high temperatures, and are comparatively intolerant of heavy foot traffic. Like Kentucky bluegrass, they do poorly if persistently cut too short.

Sheep Fescue *(F. ovin)*

Sheep fescue is so similar in appearance to red fescue, it takes an expert botanist to identify the difference. The similarity, however, is a considerable coincidence, because this grass is not a native but an alien species to Canada. The base of the blade sheath is white as opposed to red; other differential characteristics are of interest only to experts.

Left in its natural state, sheep fescue does not grow as high as *F. rubra* but it is even more tolerant of poor, sandy soils than its cousin. It is this characteristic which allows sheep fescue to be used for the establishment of lawns in poor, sandy terrain. Sheep fescue is also favoured by sheep ranchers as a pasture grass and derives its name from this fact.

Red Fescue *(F. rubra)*

Sheep Fescue   Red fescue, sometimes known as creeping red fescue, is one of the very few lawn grasses completely tolerant of acid soil conditions like those found along the Ottawa River Valley, around Montreal and over Ontario's famous Muskoka cottage country. This grass can be somewhat less satisfactory in areas with hot, humid summers, where it is susceptible to disease. Both the common and scientific name is derived from the colour at the base of the blade sheath.

Red fescue is a highly variable native species in appearance with round somewhat wiry blades. In its natural state, it may reach as high as a metre (about three feet) on poorer and even rocky soils in full sun. Nevertheless, as has been said, it is more valued for its shade tolerance when utilized for lawns. As with all desirable lawn grasses, red fescue has the ability to spread by rhizomes or stolons. Chewing fescue (*F. rubra commutata*) is a specific variety occasionally encountered in lawn seed blends. It does not wear as well as other common lawn species but is still tolerable. Hybridizers have found in *F. rubra* a happy hunting ground and developed many cultivars.

Red fescue, as with all fescues, should be sown at a rate of two kilograms or more per hundred square metres (four and one-half pounds or more to a thousand square feet).

Tall Fescue (F. elatior)

Tall fescue is a disease-resistant fescue that, unlike most of its cousins, is able to tolerate considerable foot traffic. Thanks to this characteristic, tall fescue is often a choice for public playgrounds and parks. Unfortunately, and for unexplainable reasons, this grass is frequently cut far too short when used in such situations.

Tall fescue is not native to Canada, and was almost certainly first introduced into North America for use in pastures. It has frequently escaped from such locales to become common along roads and in vacant lands where it somewhat resembles red fescue. Tall fescue is considered important agriculturally today, and horticulturally important in lawns. Like its cousins, this grass spreads by stolons as well as by seed when left to itself.

Kentucky Bluegrass (Poa pratensis)

An immigrant from Eurasia as well as, at least in part, a native species, Kentucky bluegrass represents the classic success story. It arrived as an immigrant in North America with settlers in the eighteenth century, and since that time, has flourished over a large geographic area – particularly, as one might expect from its name, in the southern

Soccer Fan Ashes Bad for Grass

British soccer fans frequently request that when they die, their bodies should be cremated and the ashes scattered on the soccer fields of a favourite team. Manchester United reportedly receives twenty-five such requests per annum. The British Football Association (BFA), however, advises an excess of ashes is bad for the grass. BFA recommends ashes be scattered around perimeters of the soccer field rather than over the actual playing area.

Appalachians, with the limestone soils. Gardeners used to finding Kentucky bluegrass manicured into traditional lawns may be surprised to learn that it has also been widely planted as a pasture grass, and can grow to almost one metre high (three feet) under favourable conditions. Bluegrass competes with native prairie grasses. Unlike them, it grows best in cooler spring weather. Later in summer, when droughts set in, the opposite occurs, as prairie grasses grow best in the hotter months and can withstand drought better since they are deeper rooted.

Thanks to its ability to spread by stolons, bluegrass is popular in commercial sod production. Plant breeders have developed several hundred cultivars. All tolerate high summer temperatures (although they do not grow a great deal under such conditions), as well as heavy foot traffic. Bluegrass is resistant to most common diseases.

A healthy, thick lawn is achieved by sowing the seed at one to one-and-one-half kilograms per hundred square metres (two-and-three quarters to four-and-one-quarter pounds per thousand square feet) in good loam with a pH level of around 6.5, or slightly acidic. These are also the conditions in which most other garden plants flourish. Given adequate soil moisture, grass seed takes up to a month to germinate. The optimum time for sowing is late summer. Following establishment, the lawn requires careful attention, with regular mowing, irrigation, fertilization, aeration and, if necessary, dethatching. Although a few cultivars are claimed to withstand some shade, Kentucky bluegrasses generally only do well when they receive a minimum of six hours full sun every day.

Kentucky bluegrass cultivars can withstand high summer temperatures, but the preferred range is lower: best growth is in late spring and early summer for most of Canada. Growth slows in July and August. The cooler fall months favour growth again, but not to the same extent as spring. Generally, the higher level of nutrient requirements will be in spring and fall. Modern fertilization programmes usually recommend application mid-to late spring, repeating in late summer or early fall. Fertilizing in the height of summer is useless and a waste.

The main reason for poor performance of Kentucky bluegrasses is "scalping" or cutting the lawn too low. Maintain this grass at a minimum of five centimetres (two inches) high except for the final mowing of the year when it can be reduced to one and one quarter centimetres (one-half inch) to

Kentucky bluegrass

discourage disease problems the following spring. Improper watering or total lack of water is another common source of miserable performance. Two and one-half centimetres (one inch) of water a week are called for, applied in two bursts, three days apart, unless there are heavy and prolonged rains. If grass clippings are chopped finely by a mulching attachment on the lawn mower there will be less call for fertilizer, but some will still be required. There are common and easily obtainable commercial sources of "natural" as well as "chemical" nutrients. The choice is a personal one, but do note that careless and improper use of both chemical and natural fertilizers can pollute.

OTHER GRASSES

Elephant Grass (Typha elephantina)

A tall reed-grass from India, *Typha elephantina*, is used there for manufacturing various forms of ropes and baskets.

Vetiver Grass

A tropical Asian grass, now grown commercially in Florida as well as India and Sri Lanka for its aromatic roots, which were traditionally woven into mats, screens and baskets. Today the essential oil is much in demand by the cosmetic and perfume industries.

Eaton's Grasses

Prairie grasses named after the American botanist, Amos Eaton (1776-1842), author of the *Manual of Botany* which went through eight editions between 1817 and 1840.

Muhly Grasses

Native grasses first described by the Lutheran pastor Gotthilf Heinrich Muhlenberg (1753-1815) of Lancaster Pennsylvania and commemorated as Mulenbergia.

Panic Grasses

A native grass species of the Canadian Prairies is Scribner's Panic Grass, *Panicum scribnerianum*.

> ### Grass Indicates Murder Site
>
> *According to superstition, the grass at the site of a murder grows greener than elsewhere.*

Establishing a New Lawn

There is nothing more restful or beautiful than a lawn and trees.

Mackenzie King, *Diaries*, 17 August 1924

Some time around 1260, Albertus Magnus, Count Bollstadt, wrote about the pleasures of a well-maintained and closely trimmed lawn. The Count seems to have been a practical man, because he also advised on the proper way to establish a successful lawn, suggesting that the ground first be well cleared of weed roots. This goal, he said, could only be achieved by first digging the roots, then levelling the land, and then completely flooding it with boiling water. This practice remains an excellent one for dispatching all weeds growing between paving stones; but obtaining a sufficient quantity of bubbling water to treat a larger area thoroughly conjures up visions of boiling cauldrons pivoted atop massive castle walls. This solution does not appear very practical in modern times. The Count's narrative suggests that following such treatment, the whole area may be covered with rich turf, which should then be beaten down with wide wooden mallets.

Perceptive gardeners know good lawns require good soil and hard work at the grassroots level, as Albertus Magnus wrote over seven hundred years ago. And, his mallet treatment seems to have continued for several centuries judging by surviving paintings and written accounts of that era. One wonders why.

Unfortunately, all too often we northerners expend less than due diligence in our preparations for the establishment of a lawn. Grass depends on its underlying soil for support and once that soil is covered over with a lawn there is little anyone can do to improve its basic structure. One might say it is like being given the most succulent of foods to eat, but no house to live in.

Today, developers of most modern subdivisions simply level all the construction rubble with a bulldozer, spread some five centimetres (two inches) of so-called topsoil over the mess, then level and roll the whole with a power roller more usually utilized in the laying of asphalt. The sod is then laid. With some help from rain god, Pluvius Jupiter, maybe the heavens will deliver adequate irrigation and the sod will take, but it will not be because of any special care on the contractors' part. Contractors know that a house surrounded by grass sells faster than one that is not. They also know that most prospective buyers are not likely to dig a hole in the ground in order to inspect the quality of the lawn work.

Soil is not dirt. Dirt is what politicians and the like sweep under carpets. Soil is what plants grow in. Soil comes in over a thousand different basic types, so varied and variable that some agricultural scientists spend entire professional careers studying them.

Fortunately for us, the research can be considerably simplified. All soils overlie the "country rock" or bedrock typical of a given region. Often this bedrock is buried so deeply as to be of no further concern to us, although people residing on the Canadian Shield as well as in parts of the Atlantic Provinces and British Columbia are all too familiar with what the local rock is, as great whacking outcrops of the stuff appear regularly on residential lots. Usually, one finds several metres of subsoil layered on top of the bedrock. Subsoil is lighter in colour than the topsoil above it, because subsoil contains little or no organic matter, and is incapable of supporting growth of any kind. Over the centuries, subsoil has been eroded by various natural forces such as wind, frost and rain; it has been burrowed into by earthworms, rodents and other animals, and penetrated by plant roots. When animals and plants die, their remains are broken down by micro-organisms in the soil and added to the eroded surface. All of this forms what we call topsoil, and the process is extremely slow (by human standards), as possibly less than a centimetre forms every century.

Unfortunately topsoil is very easily destroyed. A few hours carelessness with heavy machinery can wreck the work of centuries. Erosion, especially by wind and water, is even more insidious. Most people imagine soil washes away only on steep slopes. This is simply not so: even a slope of two or three degrees can result in several tons of soil per hectare disappearing each and every year. In rural areas, topsoil runoff clogs watercourses, ponds, and lakes. In urban areas, it is a major problem for municipal engineers. Even a poorly maintained lawn reduces topsoil erosion to almost zero.

Grass requires a topsoil depth of some fifteen centimetres (six inches) in order to grow really well. Persons lucky to have such a topsoil depth on their property should remember that it may have taken up to a thousand years to form. Treat the treasure accordingly. New subdivisions, usually built on former farmland, generally do not have the original top soil, because the developer often sells it off to firms who treat, package, and finally retail it back to the homeowners in bags or by the cubic yard. New topsoil must be brought in and, although it should be deposited fifteen centimetres (six inches) deep, that seldom happens. This new topsoil should also be "black topsoil," the most preferred as per landscape specifications and richest in organic matter. Anyone who is directing new topsoil operations for his or her own home may want to consider the slight additional expense of ordering what the trade calls "triple mix." This is an equal proportion of black topsoil, sand, and composted manure, mixed together and screened to remove any large weeds, clods or collections of uncomposted matter. Sometimes one sees "black muck" being touted. This is almost one hundred percent organic soil, usually from the bottom of drained swamps and shallow lakes. Properly treat-ed, it is the stuff of a vegetable farmer's dreams, but initially, at least, it is likely to be far too acidic to support grass and most other garden plants.

Okay, so you have inherited the problems caused by careless construction and less than professional installation. The underlying topsoil is no more than a couple of inches thick, and already the turf is showing signs of even worse stress than you. One of the glories of horticulture is that there is always hope! Please turn to the chapter on renovating lawns before attempting to drown your sorrows in some-thing more potent than water.

Knowing what topsoil is, and knowing that it must be a minimum of fifteen centimetres (six inches) deep, with reasonable drainage before grass will grow well, allows the home gardener to realize the fact that the average potential lawn site requires much improvement either by seeding or by sodding before planting. Whether planting is undertaken by the gardener personally, or by a professional company, knowledge of what is necessary can save heartache and, for that matter, real pain elsewhere in the anatomy.

It is impractical to remove all existing unacceptable soil to perhaps thirty cen-timetres or a foot, replacing it with topsoil or triple mix, except in the most

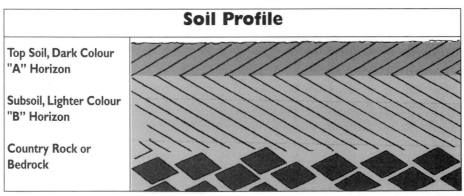

Soil Profile

Top Soil, Dark Colour "A" Horizon

Subsoil, Lighter Colour "B" Horizon

Country Rock or Bedrock

restricted areas or if you have money to burn. Such a total upheaval is occasionally required with town-house gardens, and where the owner is desirous of growing shrubs, small trees and perennials. Townhouse gardens, while horticulturally challeng-ing, are seldom large enough to warrant a lawn.

Cultivate your soil as thoroughly and as deeply as possible while incorporating into it very large quantities of composted organic matter. The best way to accomplish this integration is either by hand digging or by using a full-size farm tractor and plough. Rototillers are vastly overrated for this task. The best of them, tractor mounted, seldom penetrate below twenty centimetres (eight inches). In my opinion, those with front-mounted tines (which are frequently sold or rented to home gar-deners) are little more than fancy and expensive toys. Front-mounted rototillers are seldom capable of cultivating more than ten centimetres (four inches) deep, and then only in fairly soft and often formerly cultivated soil. The pounding they inflict upon the soil is worse, as it reduces the structure critical to good plant growth, lawns included.

Large landscape contracting companies have tractor and plough rentals and can do an excellent job on the average size suburban lot in an hour or so. Unless you are prepared for some hard physical labour, this is the only thorough way to prepare the existing soil. Hand digging is, however, an excellent substitute for jogging, tennis, and similar sports, and results in a very tangible asset – a beautiful garden.

In 1919, the Massey Foundation funded a central quadrangle covered with grass for the University of Toronto Student's Union. This quadrangle is also located over what is the now famous Hart House Theatre. Raymond Massey, actor and scion of the Massey family, claims in his autobiography A Thousand Different Lives *(1979), that Hart House is the only theatre he knows with a lawn on its roof.*

Locate a reliable source of composted, screened manure a couple of weeks prior to digging or ploughing. Your local garden centre will often be able to recommend a supplier, or you can inquire of friends and neighbours. When you've located your source, inform him or her of the area you wish to cover and the coverage depth, at least seven centimetres or about three inches. In many areas, local laws and/or insurance cover-age prevent manure suppliers from dumping directly on your lawn or on the street. Your precious load of compost has to be dumped in the

The American Velvet Robe

Let your lawn be your home's velvet robe, and your flowers its not too promiscuous decorations

Frank C. Scott, The Art of Beautifying Suburban Home Grounds *(1879)*

driveway. Make sure then that delivery is made early on a day when you will be home ready, willing, and able to spread it. Many a do-it-yourself homeowner has arrived home after a tough day at work, only to find the driveway blocked by several cubic yards of composted manure. Then comes the rush to change into old clothing, rent or borrow a heavy construction wheelbarrow while trying to make sufficient room to park the car. And naturally, usually the municipality chooses to commence a blitz on illegal overnight street parking that very same day.

Using a square-nosed shovel, the implement of choice, you should spread the compost evenly across your plot a week before digging or ploughing. There is every chance that it will contain a proportion of weed seeds, however well composted. Much can be accomplished in seven days including the germination of most weed seeds. They can then be eliminated by burial.

If you choose to have your area professionally ploughed, just sit back and allow the operator to do the job, ensuring only that he or she does not ricochet off any mature trees, damaging the bark. Some gardeners like to add bone meal fertilizer in generous quantities before the ploughing takes place. The theory behind this is that bone meal is an excellent natural source of phosphates, an essential nutrient for all plants, including grasses. Bone meal takes some time to break down and moves very, very slowly through the soil when it is scattered on the surface. Burying it deeper will encourage roots to penetrate more deeply into the soil, seeking out the fertilizer supply. After the ploughing is finished, use a gravel rake to level the soil roughly. Take the opportunity to remove all debris – construction rubble, bits of scrap lumber, roots, stones and the like.

Let the soil lie fallow for another week so the exposed weed seeds will germinate. Weed seeds can survive in the soil for decades, if not a century and more. They germinate only when disturbed and raised into the top fraction (less than two and one-half centimetres or one inch) of the soil layer. Leaving the soil exposed also allows birds and other predators to have a feast on pests, their larvae and eggs.

If you live in a suburban or even urban area, the idea of ploughing with a tractor is not to be considered And we've already pointed out that rototillers are not recommended and why. You'll have to prepare your plot in the time. honoured way of the craftsman, by hand or with a spade (what procrastinating bureaucrats would call an implement for the inversion of soil). Choose a square-nosed spade as it does a cleaner job in most situations. Use a pointed-nosed spade when there are many tree or shrub roots to be cut through. Sharpen the business end of whatever your chosen tool is with a flat file prior to commencing work. This simple improvement makes the difference between hard but steady work and utter torture.

The Eurasian continent houses two civilizations, the English and the Chinese, both of whom have had an immense influence on their neighbours, particularly in gardening. The Chinese invented the first wheelbarrow about two millennia ago – although the western Europeans took another thousand years to discover its advantages. The English did not invent the spade, but they took to it like true gardeners, although they called this new tool a "spit." Today we still talk about a "spit deep" or one spade's depth. Deep, regular cultivation is one of the main secrets of the rich soils found in both Chinese and English horticulture. These soils are not achieved without work, without digging two spits deep all around. Today, the more genteel folk call this practice "double digging."

Begin "double digging" by neatly excavating one end of the area to be cultivated to a spit's depth. Continue excavating for the entire width of lawn. If you are landscaping the whole garden completely, go ahead and dig the whole area up – flower beds, shrubbery, everything, including the lawn. You will need to come back about forty-two centimetres, or sixteen and one-half inches (two good spade-loads) from your working end. Now remove the excavated soil to the far end making sure that all debris is picked out. Now at the furthest end, at the bottom of the trench already created, dig a second spit down and about twenty-two centimetres (nine inches) back. Deposit this soil with the rest. You should now have an irregular hole which resembles a set of steps. Sprinkle a generous amount of bone meal fertilizer and then seven centimetres (three inches) of composted manure over the bottom of the lowest trench and fork it. Sprinkle the same mixture on top of the second step and turn that on top of the first. Now move back to the surface and begin to create another step by spreading the compost and bone meal on the next line, twenty-two centimetres (nine inches) back from the first, at grade level. Turn that soil over on top of the first section dug. You are now back where you started, with a double step. Keep repeating this process until you reach the other end of your plot. You can use the soil excavated first to backfill the final section. Turn any annual weeds you encounter completely under; remove all perennial weed roots and destroy them. The final move will be to rake the soil roughly level. If possible, slope your plot as gently as possible away from the house. A grade of two percent (one quarter-inch over one foot) is acceptable. Remember that anything over thirty degrees is too steep to be maintained with turf.

Every professional horticulturist performs the "double digging" and sometimes even "triple dig-

ging" process at least once in his/her career, usually while undergoing basic training for his/her future profession. Anybody who manages a successful double digging project must be dedicated. Interestingly enough, many horticulturists in later
life write about the process considerably more often than they do it.

Leave the plot alone for a week to allow for settling, weed seed germination,
and bug elimination. Then adjust the pH as necessary. A simple pH test kit, available at garden centres and science stores, will determine if your soil's acidity/alka-
linity is within the 6.0 to 7.0 range or neutral. Almost all soil problems happen
when there is too much acidity. Application of finely ground dolomitic limestone
will adjust pH levels upwards. Raising a hundred square metres (one thousand
square feet) up 1.0 pH takes varying weights of limestone, dependent upon the
nature of the underlying soil:

sandy soils	10 kg (22 lb.)
good loam	20 kg (44 lb.)
clay soils	30 kg (66 lb.)

The easiest and most accurate way to apply dolomitic limestone is with an
ordinary fertilizer spreader. If you cannot obtain dolomitic limestone which, as a
bonus, contains the secondary nutrient magnesium (Mg), other horticultural limes
will suffice, though they will not have the beneficial side effects. Always apply
lime at least a week before laying sod or seeding.

Roll the entire cultivated area with a lawn roller twelve percent (one-eighth)
filled with water immediately prior to sowing grass seed or laying the sod. Next,
use a gravel rake, to work the soil over again, very lightly just enough to create a
fine tilth in the top centimetre or quarter-inch. This will permit easy root penetra-

tion for sod and a good seedbed
for sowing. Use the roller again
following seeding to press the
seed into the soil.

Germinated weeds and young
plants both benefit from higher
levels of phosphorous (P) in the
form of absorbable phosphate.
Apply either a commercial
phosphate preparation, or
superphosphate at the rate of
two kilograms (four and one-
half pounds) per hundred
square metres (one thousand
square feet) just hours before
you plan to seed or sod. This

mixture should be raked in lightly, never dug under.

You may have noticed a great many wriggly things during ploughing or digging. These creepy-crawlies and general wild life you wish didn't exist in your garden are almost all beneficial, despite the fact that only Boris Karloff could love them. Some are even predators of the bad guys, which are often plump white maggots with dark brown or black heads called, collectively, white grubs. White grubs chomp on plant roots, including grasses. They are not found in British Columbia where they have been replaced by leatherjackets, larvae of an illegal immigrant, the European crane fly. Leatherjackets also occur in Nova Scotia, where they hopped ship in Cape Breton. Recently they have cropped up in Ontario's fabled Golden Horseshoe. Leatherjackets also feast on grass roots, where they look like little dirty grey spindles. Their name comes from their tough hides. There are no recognized effective natural controls for these little blighters, a swift and expensive round of chemical assassination is called for.

Now the basic question concerning a new lawn is usually whether to seed or sod. Which is better? There are no hard and fast rules. Your choice depends upon your personal desire and, to some extent, the depth of your pocketbook.

Sodding provides an instant lawn. In fact in the West, several companies use just the word "instant" in their names. Interestingly enough, out on the West Coast, especially in British Columbia, "Ma Bell" does not use the word sod in her "Yellow Pages," but rather "turf." In all fairness, "turf" is a very old English word, with the plural form "turves" (now obsolete). By whatever name you want to call it, sodding provides fast, fast relief from erosion, as well as for those who work with it: "the sons of soil covered with tons of soil" (P.G. Wodehouse).

Sod can be used for sun bathing and holding garden parties within just two

or three weeks following installation, perhaps even less. Your kids can even stay home and play on it. Sod can be laid anytime except during the very depths of winter as long as there is sufficient water to supply irrigation. If the sod companies can cut it, you can lay it.

But sodding is expensive compared to seeding, and entails considerably heavier work. Good sod runs well over $2 a square yard, and is supplied to the retail trade in rolls eighteen inches by six feet, metric notwithstanding. A single roll weighs about thirty pounds with average moisture content. If it has been raining, this weight can increase to as much as seventy-five pounds for the first roll, and each becomes progressively heavier to lift . . . or at least it seems that way. And lifted it must be. Sod should be laid within twenty-four hours of delivery. This is not work suggested for anyone suffering from a bad back. Nor are you able to choose precisely the blend of grasses you might desire for your particular situation. Most sod companies offer two choices: a sun sod or a shade sod. If your lawn area has both sun and shade, choose turf suitable for the latter. Shade sod will also do well in sun, whereas sod blended for sun definitely does not appreciate shaded conditions. Of course any sod company worth its name grows a product most suitable for that portion of the country it services. Many companies have farms dotted all over a province, or even an entire, very wide band of the country.

Seed, on the other hand, offers almost limitless choices as to the cultivars or species to be purchased already blended. It may be possible to mix your own seed blend, particularly when purchasing on a larger scale. Many garden centres, nurseries, and seed-catalogue companies offer house custom blends suitable for those areas in which they are located or to which they sell. These special blends are probably the best bet for those wishing the least problems. The seed is usually of good-to-excellent quality and, while not cheap, usually contains no, or minuscule, amounts of hulls, weed seeds, and rogue grasses.

However, with the exception of the extremely cool, moist parts of Canada, like the Maritimes and the Pacific Coast, grass seed may only be sown in late summer or possibly with some luck, in mid- to late spring, with any hope of good germination and survival. Grass germinates best when the days are warm and the nights cool, and when plenty of moisture is available. Canada's notoriously short springs where the temperature within a month can fluctuate between frost warnings to over 25C days with blazing sun, will cause catastrophic change to lawns newly established from seed. It takes two or three months before a newly seeded lawn can be used, which means that foot traffic during that time must be strictly prohibited. The soil must be gently watered on a daily basis, at least for the first four weeks. These restrictions can cause real problems if a lawn from seed is desired for a vacation property only occupied on weekends. Nevertheless, a seeded lawn is easier on both pocketbook and back, while the blends available can be fine-tuned for the best possible results.

The choice is yours. Families with small children, those with little time to spend, or people not in robust health will find sod the most satisfactory answer. And today there are few places a sod truck cannot reach – outside of perhaps some Arctic communities, although even there one should be prepared for surprises as civilization continues its remorseless advance. People who live in truly remote areas, or those who wish for the ultimate lawn, might be advised to choose seed. In this modern world, seeded lawns are far outnumbered by turf lovers, and it is the latter to which we will now turn our attention.

When laying sod, keep two critical things in mind: lay within twenty-four hours of delivery, preferably the day of delivery; and make sure your turf receives a complete drenching within an hour of being installed. Delivery of your sod must be carefully coordinated with the supply company. Order directly from the grower for all projects of any size. An intermediary may delay delivery. One may be required to have cash, cheque or credit card ready when the sod is delivered, depending on the company. However, the author has dealt for many years with a very large sod company which has never demanded that anyone be around at all for delivery. More than one customer has woken up on a bright cheerful Saturday morning to find that the sod truck quietly dropped off the order at five in the morning, and stuck the invoice in the mailbox. Gardeners, professional as well as amateur, are trusting sorts.

Usually a crew of four adults and sturdy (and willing) youths is required to lay sod. Three people carry the sod and one lays it. There is no practical way to clean clothing completely following this work and sturdy footwear is advisable since heavy rolls and sharp tools are the name of the game. Once under way and in the swing, an amateur crew of four can lay ninety-three to one hundred and eighty six square metres (one thousand to two thousand square feet) in about three hours, but coverage will drop considerably after this effort. It is best to water sod almost as soon as it is laid, so a fifth pair of arms to hold the hose is a distinct advantage both for the grass and for the thirsty. Laying is hot, hard, and dirty work – but also peculiarly satisfying as the lawn takes shape before your very eyes.

Sods are laid brick fashion, with the joints overlapping each other, never opposite. Never, ever bend sod to shape, although you may allow a small amount to overflow onto the surrounding paths or beds. Incidentally, if you desire curved edges for these latter, use your garden hose to outline such. Cord or string will blow in the wind, twist or be tripped over, even without the help of your dog chasing the neighbour's cat through it. Use a turf cutter, that tool with the curved blade and long handle, to trim the sod back when all is completed.

Use the odds and ends that result for patching small holes, or place them upside down in piles to make some of the best old-fashioned soil for filling containers and planters. It is always better to have slightly too much sod, rather than too little. If there are any gaps between strips of sod, you can fill with the leftover scraps, or use sterilized potting soil from your local garden centre. Ordinary garden soil from the nearest flower bed probably has a healthy dose of weed seed, which is likely to cause botheration, frustration and intemperate language when it germinates. For your final finishing touch, roll the lawn once again with the roller one-eighth filled with water.

The longer you can keep off your newly-laid sod, the better, especially if it is being watered heavily. If your new sodded area is not already fenced, hammer in five by five centimetre (two by two inch) stakes and stretch strong, brightly coloured twine between them. The same, incidentally, applies to any newly-seeded lawn. Restrain yourself from the new lawn for at least a week. Two weeks would be even better, although it is usually more like a matter of days before the lawn is subject to use. Allow the grass to grow at least seven and one-half centimetres (three inches), before reducing to five centimetres (two inches) with a very sharp mower. Sod laid in summer does not usually require fertilization that fall.

Do not mow seeded lawns until they are at least seven and one-half to nine centimetres (three to four inches) high, and make sure you use a very sharp mower. It should not be necessary to fertilize late summer sown lawns in fall of the same year as this practice is likely to "burn" the grass.

Now take advantage of your new lawn. Don't feel embarrassed. It is politically correct. Move a chair out into the shade, ensure a suitable beverage is close to hand and read the rest of this book. Others can cultivate the rest of the garden. As an expert in that most vital part of the horticultural scene, the lawn, it is your job to stay in touch with all the latest developments, new materials, and advanced techniques. This all takes time, careful study, and careful contemplation in the shade.

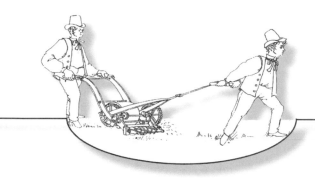

Lawn Maintenance

Flower beds are often best set in grass, and those that care to see them will approach them quite as readily on grass as on hard walks.

William Robinson, prolific English garden writer (1883)

Why can't we invent a grass which needs no care? We can, and it's been done – Astroturf. Not only does Astroturf cost more than grass to install and to lay, but apparently it also produces some most interesting and unique injuries, according to several noted sports injury experts.

And it was perhaps with that fact in mind that, when the United States hosted the World Soccer Tournament in an indoor stadium in Pontiac, Michigan, they threw out the artificial turf and installed real grass.

When the late Shah of Iran celebrated the anniversary of his country by building a new golf course for the use of visiting dignitaries and their handlers, the turf was airlifted from France.

Lawns need regular care to maintain them in good shape. Good care is not particularly difficult, nor does it take a great deal of time. Watch how fast garden maintenance contractors can complete the work. Of course, they make it look easy because they are experts, but here is a summary of how it is done:

- maintain grass at a height of five centimetres (two inches) spring through fall
- do not remove more than two-thirds the total height at any one time
- mow regularly until the grass stops growing in fall
- the final mowing should reduce the height of the grass to just over one centimetre (one-half inch) in height
- water every three days applying just over one centimetre (one-half inch) each time. Leaving the sprinkler on for about an hour at average municipal water pressure achieves this result, as does a prolonged heavy rain. The best time to water is the middle of the night, but remember to use a timer on the faucet
- fertilize in mid-to late spring and again in late summer or early fall
- apply a light top-dressing of clean, weed-free compost about the same time
- aerate in late spring and again in early fall
- rake fallen tree leaves off the lawn in fall
- hand dig the odd weed

Planning a garden party, wedding reception, or other major event in your garden and you haven't time to get the beds in really good condition? Don't worry! Mow your lawn. Then take the turf edger to trim the edges of your flower bed cleanly and vertically, as well as those areas where lawn meets walkways and/or driveways.

Mowing

Maintenance Mowing Heights			
	Rough Lawn	**Normal Lawn**	**Winter Lawn**
4 inches			
3 inches			
2 inches			
1 inch			
	larger, usually rural properties	most home lawns	reduce to in late fall

Height

The best and most weed-free home lawns are never cut shorter than five centimetres (two inches) until the final cut of the season when the height is reduced to just over a centimetre or half-inch. Couple this maxim with the practice of never removing more than two-thirds of the total grass blade length at one time and your lawn will become so thick that weeds are literally choked out. And, grass roots will grow very long, enabling your lawn to withstand droughts better than its scalped neighbour next door. It is a simple fact that grass regularly cut short will have equally abbreviated roots.

Reducing height of your grass on the final cut late in the year is preferable because it removes the possibility of dead grass impeding new growth the following spring. Grass kept very short over winter is almost always found to be less prone to attack by pests and diseases the following season.

Safety

Always police the lawn prior to mowing. Secure dog, children, and other wildlife. Make sure the neighbour's dog (of course, it is never your own) has not left distressing contributions to be discovered only after your mower has passed over them. Pick up all debris which might turn into dangerous missiles when hit by the mower: stones, pieces of bark mulch, and even large twigs can be hurled with enormous force by mower blades (which may move at speeds approaching three hundred and forty kilometres or two hundred miles an hour in a rotary model).

Remember that the power cord on electric mowers is a potential danger. Make sure it stays to the side on which the grass has already been cut. Never, ever mow with a cord which is worn, or casually repaired, or both.

Slopes can be lethal. Any slope over thirty degrees should be replanted with alternate ground cover which does not require mowing. Even banks less steep are dangerous when slightly wet, or when your lawn has clover mixed in with the grass.

Mowers

Because we provide a thorough discussion of the pros and cons of various mowers in Chapter 8, we will merely note here that hand-pushed reel mowers give a cut far superior to all other alternatives. Moreover, they do not pollute, and they offer excellent exercise. Many urban and suburban lawns can be maintained using these machines.

Larger lawns, of course, require motorized mowers. You may consider an electric-powered rotary model for suburban use, but the classic gas-engine rotary walk behind mower will be most people's choice. Only the very largest of properties requires a ride-on mower, and remember, a miniature tractor is a better choice because it can be used for other chores – like snow ploughing in winter.

Clippings

Lawn clippings should be left on the lawn to return nutrients to the soil. You must make sure they are shredded very finely. Some experts claim that it is possible to reduce fertilizer applications, whether chemical or natural, by up to thirty percent, when lawn clippings are not removed. This sounds great, and is great. But the clippings must be shredded very, very finely. This process requires that you either purchase a mulching lawn mower, or change your cutting blade to one designed to do this job.

There is always the temptation to dump a pile of clippings into the nearest flower bed as a mulch. This is a no no! Clippings will ferment and attract ants: they also exclude air from the soil and use up valuable nitrates while breaking down in a process known as denitrification. Mix clippings with other organic waste matter and compost. On rare occasions, when disease is present, it will be absolutely necessary to collect and bag clippings for disposal. The compost will not serve as a suitable depository because it does not reach a high enough and suitably sustained temperature to destroy the spores.

Watering

Improper mowing of grass is the most common reason for poor lawns, but incorrect watering runs a close second. Most people water too little and too often. Standing on your porch with the hose and spraying the lawn may cool you down, but it spells disaster for your grass. The lawn receives little water, most of which fails to penetrate the soil: its roots grow close to the surface where they are then prone to the first drought. Lawns rarely fully recover from this treatment. Properly timed, sensible watering uses less water to better effect and is easier on all concerned.

Water every three days, unless there is prolonged torrential rain. Spring usually has a water reservoir from winter and the soil will remain moist for several weeks even without rain. Some knowledgeable gardeners like to test the soil using moisture meters sold for checking indoor plants.

Each water application should result in about one centimetre (one-half inch) all over the lawn. Incidentally, the rest of your garden, particularly your vegetables, will benefit from this schedule as well. You can determine when the correct water amount has been reached by marking a line around an empty tin can using a chinagraph or indelible pen. Position the can about halfway across the sprinkler pattern. Do not use a glass jar: if it is accidentally broken, you will find it almost impossible to clear away all the shards. They will remain a permanent hazard to bare feet or to your mower. Alternatively you can forget about measuring, but leave the sprinkler running for an hour, and that, at average municipal water pressure, should disseminate the required amount.

The best time to water is during the middle of night, and no, you do not have to interrupt your sleep. Most garden centres and hardware stores sell simple timers which attach to the faucet. These may turn on the water every few days or more through complex timing cycles, depending largely upon the price. Most run on small batteries and have locks to secure them. Watering in the middle of the night means there will be more pressure in the mains, and less lost through evaporation. Even more importantly, night watering causes fewer problems with disease. If you water late in the afternoon or during early evening, grass foliage and that of other plants remain wet as night falls. The temperature usually drops, and epidermal cells chill, which creates an opportunity for fungal spores to penetrate. You have probably noticed that old-fashioned common lilac bushes become covered in a whitish powder in late spring and early fall. This mildew is encouraged by warm humid days and cool, damp nights. This is only one example, although perhaps the most obvious, of the diseases caused by incorrect irrigation.

Watering in the middle of the night also helps control insect pests. These move slowly in the lower temperatures, and when hit by the water, they can lose their grip and fall. Even when not injured by the rapid and moist descent, these creatures are rarely able to climb back onto the host plant. Raccoons, skunks, and your neighbour's visiting tomcat are other nocturnal garden visitors which thoroughly dislike a sudden dowsing.

The preferred sprinkler model for small and medium-size lawns is an oscillating one. This sweeps backwards and forwards, irrigating either a rectangular or square area depending upon the setting chosen. Sprinklers manufactured by "Melnor" are highly recommended because some models come with a built-in timer. These also are more economical than those manufactured in Europe and imported into Canada (and which do not usually have a timing feature). Larger properties require a pulsating sprinkler of the type commonly used for municipal parks and some commercial properties. Since these tools apply water in a circular pattern, there is inevitably some overlap and thus a slightly uneven application. Some of the more powerful models throw water to a remarkable distance, even on lower pressures. Some consumer models come designed as a helicopter or as a fire hydrant. As yet there are no sprinkling pink flamingoes!

In-Ground Sprinkler Systems

Even with today's do-it-yourself kits, any well-designed professionally-installed in-ground sprinkler system will run into the low thousands of dollars at the very least, and perhaps a good deal more. South of the border, down Washington way, the ground is unlikely to freeze several feet deep every winter as it does everywhere here in the north, except in the mildest parts of Canada. In areas where the ground freezes, the plumbing must be more rugged and properly selected, installed to withstand such extremes. The system should also be drained or cleared with compressed air in late fall.

An in-ground sprinkler system is usually installed in the entire garden, with the "emitters," or actual spray heads, on short poles in shrubbery. Lawns and flower beds alongside pathways are usually serviced by "pop-up" type heads, which emerge from their underground lairs only when the pressure of water signals the commencement of watering. The pressure in turn is controlled by a timer. In theory, an in-ground system means that you will never again have to worry about watering your garden at the right time, with the right amount of water. In practice, like everything mechanical, sooner or later something in an in-ground system will fail. It is only fair to add that those systems professionally

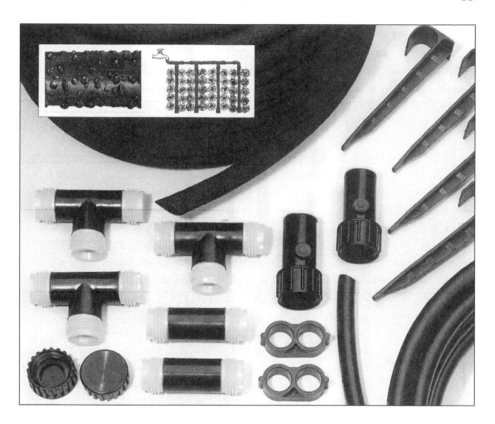

installed by reputable companies are considerably more trouble-free than almost any home device. Gardeners with extremely busy schedules, or people who are away from home often for several days or even weeks at a time, will find these systems virtually indispensable. Other consumers will wish to balance the obviously high expense against the cost and inconvenience caused by using a conventional hose and sprinkler, perhaps with a timer attached to the faucet.

Most sprinkler companies are loathe to make any kind of cost and installation estimate until they have had the chance to examine professionally prepared landscape plans. Sometimes they even want to see the finished planting. Insertion of sprinkler plumbing and the positioning of emitters does not necessarily have to take place before lawns, shrubs and perennials are all growing in their assigned places.

Most landscape contractors invariably have reputable sprinkler system installers with whom they have worked previously. If you are planning to install such a system in an already established landscape, find out if any of your neighbours have such a system and who they used. Most professionals are members of a provincial or regional landscape trades association, and use straightforward contracts which are not loaded with legalese. Most will be happy to supply references and close by addresses for other contracts they have completed.

Fertilizing
Why Fertilize Anyway?

Allan is a grass person. Too bad for him. Every year the grass, without fail, would grow withered, brown and weedy while our neighbours' grass prospered. I read somewhere that the British ambassador had airlifted elephant dung to fertilize his grass.   Sondra Gottlieb, Canadian Embassy, Washington (1990)

Mrs. Gottlieb is incorrect. The British Ambassador may, indeed, have flown in carefully composted elephant manure but never, ever for his Washington lawn. It would have been used for his trees. Elephant manure is a famous method of ensuring strong trunks, and it is most definitely a natural fertilizer, to which topic we will return shortly.

Every living thing requires nutrients in order to survive. Every living thing also requires a balanced diet to flourish. Plants obtain a large proportion of their requirements from the air, utilizing sunlight in the unique process known as photosynthesis on which all life on this planet depends. Plants absorb the balance of their requirements as minerals dissolve in water held in the soil.

There are three minerals which must be obtained in comparatively large amounts: nitrates, used in photosynthesis and vital to the green parts of the plant; phosphates, important to young plants as well as to mature plants for the formation of flowers (hence, fruits and seeds); and potassium, used particularly in roots. These minerals are expressed in scientific shorthand by the capital letters N (nitrogen), P (phosphate), and K (potassium). Experienced gardeners often will be heard talking blithely about NPK levels. Any plants grown principally for foliage, such as grasses or many houseplants, will require higher levels of nitrates (the dissolvable form of nitrogen) while flowering plants have an increased demand for phosphates.

These minerals are usually known as the "macro nutrients" or, in older reference works, as the "major nutrients." Three other chemical elements are required in somewhat lesser amounts and are, therefore, logically known as the "secondary nutrients." These are sulphur (S), magnesium (Mg), and calcium (Ca). It is not recommended that the home gardener try to adjust levels of any of these elements in the soil. Sulphur helps to "green up" the foliage but also acidifies soil when overused. Magnesium is critical in photosynthesis and is rarely found wanting in

> *Half the interest of a garden is the constant exercising of the imagination.*
> Mrs. C. W. Earle, 19th century
> English gardener

soil. Calcium is, of course, found in lime as well as egg shells. Granny may have known a thing or two when she pounded her eggshells up to add to her garden. Scattering eggshell residue is less easy for lawns and may result in some odd looks from your neighbours.

Finally, some half-dozen other nutrients are required in very minute quantities: these are known as the "micro nutrients." They are rarely lacking in the soil and if they are, as perhaps in some commercial farming operations, they are usually applied at a very few kilograms per hectare (pounds per acre). Anything more may, can, and usually does poison the soil permanently for any kind of plant growth.

So it's easy, isn't it? All you need to do is apply a nicely balanced diet to grass, a diet consisting mainly of nitrates but balanced with other nutrients, and everything will be a bed of roses. Nothing is that simple. There is yet another grub awaiting us in the grass catcher.

PH is what the university trained horticultural graduate calls the potential hydrogen ion theory. The rest of us, with instant recognition from television shampoo commercials, know it more prosaically as acidity and alkalinity. Reduced to its barest level, the pH factor means that if the soil, or "growing medium" to the graduate horticulturist, is not close to the optimum pH level, then grass or any other plants for that matter, cannot absorb the necessary nutrients.

PH level is measured on a scale of one to fourteen. The midway point, seven, is

Lawn Nutrients

Chemical Symbol Macro Nutrients	Common Name	Notes
N	Nitrogen	present in chlorophyll, phospholipids, proteins and nucleic acids (DNA, RNA) – also in some vitamins and all hormones
P	Phosphorus	found in all proteins, phospholipids, enzymes, sugar phosphates, nucleic acids, nucleotides
K	Potassium	influences stomata control, absorption and movement of other nutrients through the grass, also involved in the enzyme systems
Secondary Nutrients		
Ca	Calcium	cements cell walls
S	Sulphur	present in chloroplasts
Mg	Magnesium	plays a central role in photosynthesis
Micro Nutrients		
B	Boron	
Cl	Chlorine	
Cu	Copper	
Fe	Iron	
Mn	Manganese	
Mo	Molybdenum	
Ni	Nickel	
Zn	Zinc	

> *We cannot command Mother Nature except by obeying her*
>
> Frances Bacon

neutral. Anything less than seven is considered acidic, anything above it, alkaline. It is important to realize that the pH scale is logarithmic so that pH 5.0 is not double the acidity of 6.0 but ten times its measure, while 4.0 would be one hundred times as acidic. Vinegar is about pH 3.0, as is acid rain.

Most garden plants, including grasses, will absorb the dissolved minerals they require at pH levels of around 6.0. The famous Kentucky bluegrasses flourish at such levels. Various species of fescues are preferred where the soil is more acidic. If rhododendrons, kalmias, and bearberry flourish in your garden without any special care or attention, the underlying soils are almost certainly acidic. Clematis and the perennial gypsophila (baby's breath) prefer alkaline conditions. Older lawns which have been heavily fertilized with chemical-based fertilizers for many years (particularly in liquid form) are apt to have an underlying base of acidic soil. Acidic conditions mean grass has impaired ability to take up nutrients from the soil. Acidity also causes the heavy build-up of dead grasses known as "thatch" just above soil level. Horticultural lime applied with a spreader will adjust the pH upwards. Older gardeners are often heard referring to alkaline conditions as "sweet soil."

Certain segments of the popular gardening press and some professionals make much of pH, although, amazingly enough, these same people often seem to be involved in the marketing of test kits or laboratory services. Simple pH kits are available from science hobby stores and garden centres, and these will give an acceptable reading of pH levels. Most are under ten dollars and marvelous fun to use, especially with children around. You can show kids how vinegar turns the test solution acid, but be careful if you use baking powder (as is sometimes suggested) for an alkaline indication because foaming may occur. Whether the cheaper pH meters, those similar in appearance to the meters used to test moisture in house plants pots, really work or not is controversial. Professional meters are available. These cost several hundred dollars. Even the Romans knew about sweet soils, and the reverse, "sour" soils. They recommended tasting the soil to determine conditions. Tasting was still recommended at some highly respected horticultural colleges in the 1950s, however, given the vast increase in the canine population, as well as modern concerns regarding pollution, such practice is discouraged today.

The use of "chemical" versus "natural" fertilizers is an on-going controversy. Chemical advocates point out that urea, a common constituent of some fertilizers and a source of nitrates, was first isolated in the nineteenth century from urine, a natural source (hence the name). Chemical engineers have duplicated urea artificially with such skill that it is literally impossible to tell the natural from the artificial. So, then, what exactly is "natural?" And what about the sprinkling of blood meal fertilizer, another excellent source of nitrates, on your lawn weekly, or semi-weekly to discourage squirrels. Does this practice also pollute the environment?

Facts of Fertilizer

Weight of Bag

Company Name/Logo

Brand Name

N-P-K Ratio must appear by law

You don't expect them to say that it is low quality, do you?

If it's being sold here, why would it be for anywhere else?

Application Instructions, follow the rate recommendations exactly; the number of times will always be the maximum needed

Analysis: These are the true amounts available to the grasses, not all the contents necessarily are just that

20 KG

PRIME MINISTER'S CHOICE

SUPER SOD

Lawn Fertilizer

18 - 7 - 7

High Quality Granular Fertilizer
Specially Formulated for Canadian Lawns

apply at a rate of 10 kg per 100 sq. m.
twice in spring and again in fall

Guaranteed Minimum Analysis:
Total Nitrogen (N) 18%
Available Phosphoric Acid (P2O5) 7%
Soluble Potash K2O 7%

Prime Minister's Choice Fertilizers, 24 Sussex Drive, Ottawa, Ontario

Company Name and Address

"Chemical" or "Natural" if it is not stated it is almost certainly "Chemical"

The advocates of all-natural fertilizers hop down from their bicycles to point out that the use of chemical-formulated lawn fertilizers turns the soil more acidic, reducing the micro-organism population. Liquid fertilizers are the worse offenders they say, and the increased popularity of these preparations has been shown to increase the thatch found in lawns.

I plunk down my gardening dollars for the fertilizers which give me the best sustained results. One of the oldest is "Milorganite," which has been around since the 1920s. One major reason for the continued success of this product is the fact that greens keepers in charge of golf courses use it constantly. You may have suspected that golf courses are so doused with chemical cocktails that golf balls are in danger of dissolving. Not so! "Milorganite" is one hundred percent natural. It is processed domestic sewage sludge from Milwaukee, Wisconsin, located on the shores of Lake Michigan. Every time Milwaukee citizens flush their toilets, they enrich both their city coffers, and millions of lawns and golf courses. Milwaukee does not allow industries to connect up to its sewers, so "Milorganite" stays chemical-free.

The Canadian firm, So-Green, now part of the Vigoro empire, has for many years sold "High Organic" for lawns. This is another highly recommended fertilizer which produces astounding results when used correctly. Its only major problem (as with "Miloganite"), is that city gardeners with small lawns must buy a large bag. Fertilizers can be kept from year to year even if they freeze: the storage facility should be dry and watertight. Note, however, fertilizers containing pesticides or herbicides do not maintain their potency from year to year.

Both "High Organic" and "Milorganite" are granular fertilizers and should be applied with a spreader. Other granular fertilizers are manufactured from natural sources likes alfalfa, a leguminous crop first raised by the Arabs and now widely grown for use in pelletized foods for agricultural livestock, pet rabbits and guinea pigs. Alfalfa has found wider dissemination as a lawn fertilizer only recently. Unfortunately I am unable to name suppliers because many are very regional and, frankly, often appear and disappear like nitrates with lightning storms.

It does not matter to your lawn grasses or to every other plant in your garden whether the nutrient molecule originated from a "chemical" or a "natural" source. The plant will absorb its fertilizer regardless. The only problem gardeners face is that of possible side effects either source may inflict upon the environment, plants and/or humans.

> *His passion was for serious gardening – pitchfork, spade, or hose in hand, stomping about the property clad only in ghastly elastic swim trunks called "wickies" and a proper tall opera hat.*
>
> Cynthia Lindsay on her godfather, Boris Karloff (*William Pratt*)

Composts

Let us now turn to truly rotten matters and take a long, hard look at compost. What is it? Compost is any matter which was once living, has died and has been broken down through natural processes. When we build compost heaps, or use specially designed bins or "composters," we accelerate this process from months or years into, optimally, a few weeks. Almost any household or garden waste can be used. Exceptions are metals, plastics, large quantities of paper, fat and bones which attract vermin, and dog or cat waste which can spread disease. Waste from small vegetarian pets such as gerbils, guinea pigs, and especially rabbits (along with their bedding) is exceptionally valuable for composting. The secret to good compost is mixing it into an homogenous mass, one that is neither too wet nor too dry. Add an occasional handful of horticultural lime to keep it "sweet" or slightly alkaline.

> *In order to civilize a people, it is necessary first to fix it, and this cannot be done without inducing it to cultivate the soil.*
>
> Alexis de Tocqueville

Farmyard waste, like that of cattle and sheep, is often commercially composted and sold in twenty litre (six gallon) bags. One well known firm, Hillview, even composts waste from zoo animals, selling it under the name of "Zoopoo." Following up on a successful trend, Hillview named their cattle compost "Moopoo," and gardeners are waiting breathlessly to learn what the new sheep compost will be called. Horse manure, for those living within driving distance of a stable, has always been considered the finest candidate for composting. Unfortunately mushrooms also thrive in horse manure. The result is that mushroom farms pay premium prices for the stuff. There is usually little left from race tracks for the home gardener. Some cities with mounted police forces and stables for their horses usually allow citizens to remove the manure

Facts of Fertilizer:
Effects of pH Levels on Nutrient Absorption

	4.0 (acid)	7.0 (neutral)	10.0 (alkaline)
Nitrogen (N)	poor	good	poor
Phosphorus (P)	poor	good	good
Potassium (K)	poor	good	good
Sulphur (S)	poor	good	good
Calcium (Ca)	poor	good	medium
Magnesium (Mg)	poor	medium	medium
Iron (Fe)	good	medium	poor
Manganese (Mn)	medium	good	poor
Boron (B)	medium	medium	good
Copper (Cu)	medium	medium	poor
Zinc (Zn)	medium	medium	poor
Molybdenum (Mo)	poor	medium	good

by bushel basket. Suburban and rural dwellers have the possibility of nearby riding stables. Chicken manure is known to gardeners as being very "hot" or acidic. It can burn plants. Pig manure has an extremely distinctive aroma that may leave one, as the Latin tag has it, non compost mentis.

All composts (except for chicken and pig manure) are excellent when properly broken down into a black, crumbly state. Composts can be distributed with a standard fertilizer spreader and, while having comparatively low nutrient values in themselves, they can improve the micro-organism content of the soil as well as its texture. This makes for a far healthier lawn, and one better able to absorb nutrients from other sources while resisting pathogen attack. There is some indication, in fact, that applying compost also increases the microscopic predators and parasites of various pests.

Compost should be applied at least in late spring every year and possibly again in early fall.

When to Fertilize

So why go to all this trouble anyway? Doesn't Mother Nature take care of her own in the natural state? The small voice from the back of the class raises valid queries. Actually, dear old Mother Nature is greatly overrated. She squanders vast numbers of plants in order to grow a few. How many acorns are produced by a single oak tree every year? How many grow to become mature trees? Then again, Mother Nature is not growing plants on the intensive scale that we do in the garden, nor does she demand such perfection in her results. So if we want lawns, and if we like our gardens to be orderly and healthy, regular fertilizing is required.

Modern quality fertilizers are very, very efficient. Home lawns require small dosages to remain extremely healthy as long as other cultural procedures are attended to. The process is far simpler than in former times. All one needs to do is to apply the nutrients in mid- to late spring, and again in late summer or early fall. (Gardeners demanding the ultimate in lawns may wish to fertilize twice early in the season, in both mid- and late spring, but by fall, only one application is required.)

Many experts now believe there is no need to vary the fertilizer formulation dramatically from spring to fall, although this was formerly recommended. Today a fertilizer which is appreciably

Facts of Fertilizer

In the spring of 1984 consumer columnist Ellen Roseman of The Globe and Mail *revealed that almost all fertilizer manufacturers were adding "fillers" to their products. The one major player in the game, the then-Canadian owned So-Green Inc, had, to the consternation of the industry, brought out a specific line of "No filler added." Although when interviewed, other manufacturers lambasted So-Green, Ms. Roseman established that they had followed that company's lead or were considering doing so shortly.*

higher in nitrogen than the other two macro nutrients can be safely suggested for both spring and fall use. The NPK ration which, by law, must appear on every bag, box, and bottle of fertilizer sold, will have a larger first number than the other two.

How to Fertilize

Fertilizing is done with spreaders, which we discuss in more detail in Chapter 8. Suffice to mention here that trying to apply fertilizer by hand will likely result in a lawn with complexion problems. Many garden centres will loan spreaders with the purchase of fertilizer. These may or may not be in good condition and working properly: they also may or may not be free of all traces of pesticide or herbicide distributed by the previous user. This may or may not be of concern to you.

People with smaller lawns are advised to purchase a hand-held spreader. These also work well for distributing grass seed or lime, and other granulated products.

Divide the amount of fertilizer to be applied into two even portions. Fill the hopper of the spreader with one-half of the mixture and apply it in a north-south direction on the lawn area to be fertilized. Refill and apply the second half on the same area, but in an east to west direction, to ensure completely even coverage. Dividing the fertilizer and filling your spreader should be done on a driveway – not on your lawn. Wash and dry the spreader and store it away safely for the next use or, if borrowed, return it to the garden centre.

Aeration

Lawns that have been used for many years tend to have compacted soil. This is usually more of a problem on clay-based soils, but sooner or later all lawns will suffer the same fate. Many professionals used to chuckle at garden stores which rented out powered aerators. The accompanying literature directed home gardeners to aerate twice a year. Well, it turns out those early aerators were right.

Aeration breaks up the soil's surface crust which, when formed, prevents proper air and water penetration of the soil. Water carries the nutrients required for a happy, healthy lawn. The grass must struggle to grow when soil is compacted, and simultaneously it will be challenged by various common weeds not so particular as to where they take up residence. Many severe weed infestations occur on poorly aerated turf.

For smaller

In England, it is believed that when animals eat grass, rain will arrive shortly.

lawns, it has sometimes been recommended (half in jest) that the amateur aerator don golf shoes and walk over it. This is better than doing nothing, but is still not entirely effective. A garden fork rammed down hard every thirty centimetres (twelve inches) and given a tug backwards then forwards again before being withdrawn does more good. Suburban lawn owners might wish to investigate the possibility of purchasing small hand pushed aerators. These are similar to a reel mower, but with spikes at the business end. They look positively medieval, and something like a device dreamed up by Revenue Canada for extracting still more taxes.

Purchase of a gas-powered machine can only be justified for the very largest of private estates. Renting is better, perhaps with several neighbours all chipping in and using the machine in turn. This communal approach encourages lawn pride, while helping to prevent a badly maintained lawn on the block from infecting all the others with weeds, pests, and diseases.

Like all power equipment, aerators are not toys to be used by children or irresponsible persons. Always turn off the engine, even if leaving it for a moment.

Other Maintenance

Raking Leaves

The beautiful sugar maple on your front lawn has two hundred thousand leaves. The neighbour's mighty oak which overhangs your back garden has about three times as many plus, in a bumper year, five thousand or so acorns for the squirrels to drop on unwary craniums below. Even a standard apple tree has one hundred thousand leaves. Guess who is going to have to find a solution to these come fall?

Allowing dead leaves to lie on the grass over winter is a recipe for serious lawn problems the following season. Soaked by fall rains, the leaves form a mass that excludes light and air. The result is a dead or seriously damaged lawn. Weeds, of course, are not so badly impaired, and they will flourish while your grass struggles.

Dead leaves must be removed. A leaf rake is the most neighbour-friendly tool to use for this chore. If your entire block enjoys listening to the sounds of a banshee in agony, then leaf blowers will be found ideal. Leaf blowers are appreciated so much that one major American city (Los Angeles) has totally banned them. On very large properties, you might try using your lawn mower to achieve the same effect by circling round the fallen tree leaves as you mow, throwing them into a heap.

Okay, all the leaves have been raked into a neat pile. Unfortunately your garden is small and there is no room for the size compost heap required to reduce them down. The solution is to be found with your new self-mulching mower, purchased to avoid a similar problem with grass clippings. Crank it up, manoeuvre it over the leaves, and watch it shred them so finely that you can use them to protect perennials, bulbs, herbs, and other plants through the winter, after the ground freezes.

> *All gardening is landscape painting.*
> Alexander Pope

Why not simply rake the leaves onto the flower beds and be done with it? Walk the woods and you will find the answer. Dead leaves mat down to form a wet, soggy mass. This prevents air from reaching into the soil and the resulting stagnant conditions are poor for plant growth. Thus, little will grow under a dense canopy of trees in deep woods. When leaves are finely shredded, the story changes, as they make a superb mulch which may be piled as much as fifteen centimetres (six inches) high over flower beds. Note, this should only be done after the ground starts to freeze in less clement parts of the country. Wait for the first hard frost in coastal regions. Mulch does not prevent freezing, but it assures that when the ground does freeze, it remains so throughout winter.

Freezing does not kill perennials and other plants, but the freeze-thaw-freeze-thaw cycle that the top centimetre (one-quarter or half-inch) of soil is subjected to during milder winter periods does. It is the freeze-thaw-freeze-thaw cycle that causes the familiar frost heaving, which in turn pushes plants up to expose their most tender portion, the point where the roots meet to form the "crown." Plants are particularly vulnerable in late winter and early spring, as the frost starts to come out of the ground and the freeze-thaw-freeze-thaw cycle is accelerated. Do not mulch until the first, heavy frosts, and do not be in too much of a hurry to remove the same mulch in spring.

Weed Control

There are four methods available for fast weed control:

1. removing by hand
2. selective herbicide blended with fertilizer, the familiar "weed-and-feed" approach
3. selective herbicides applied in liquid form usually as a spray
4. employing trained and licensed professionals who will probably spray selective herbicide

The best weed control procedure takes the longest: it relies solely on proper lawn culture as we have outlined here, combined with the correct mowing length, and with the immediate removal, by hand, of any weeds that do sneak in.

Renovating

*I arrived at Mailmaison and do you know what I did, and where the First
Consul had established his workroom? On one of the bowling greens. They were
all seated on the grass. It was nothing to him, with his military habits, his
riding boots, and his leather breeches. But I, in my silk breeches and silk
stockings! Can you see me sitting on that lawn? I'm crippled with
rheumatism. What a man!*   Talleyrand, French diplomat of Napoleon

S ooner of later most gardeners will inherit a neglected lawn. It may be a
matter of defeating a few too many weeds. Or grass may be growing, in the
words of Rogers and Hammerstein, "as high as an elephant's eye," or at
least a moose's eye.

The first steps to regaining control are to abide by the golden rules of
lawn care:
- Adjust mower blades so that they do not cut the grass below five centimetres (two inches) high.
- Apply just over a centimetre (one-half inch) of water every three days unless there have been prolonged rains.
- Fertilize in late spring and again in late summer or early fall with a high-nitrogen fertilizer.
- Aerate every spring and fall.

Before proceeding with any further action, take time out to survey the lawn
thoroughly. Most neglected lawns, in addition to the steps summarized above, need
pest and disease control, overseeding to fill in bare patches and thicken up the
remaining turf, dethatching to permit air, water, and nutrients to reach the soil,
and probably edging with a lawn-edging tool, also known as a turf knife.

Lawns which consist of up to sixty percent weeds can be reclaimed by cultural
methods. Very few lawns, however badly neglected, have less than forty percent
grass. If your lawn has healthy weeds you can be fairly sure that it does not have
either of two of the worse lawn pests – both are root-feeders: white grubs in the

East and leatherjackets in the West. Leatherjackets, previously known only in southwest British Columbia and parts of Nova Scotia, surfaced recently in south-central Ontario following a very mild winter. Still, it is reassuring to learn that healthy, happy weeds probably indicate no serious pests present.

So take heart. When the grass grows sparsely with patches of totally dead grass, treat it as follows. Tug on the grass gently. If it will not come up without a determined pull, then it is still attached to its roots, dead as it may look. The obvious conclusion is that something has been causing damage from above, and not below, ground. Suspect dogs and their lack of toilet training. Dog urine and excrement permanently poison the soil. The damage is not so noticeable in areas or times of the year prone to heavier rains. In those areas, however, where the ground freezes over in winter with a reasonable snow cover, frost moving out of the ground in spring signals the onset of severe damage as the frozen excrement is released to do its worst. The only cure is to dig out the soil and the destroyed turf to a minimum fifteen centimetres (six inches) depth, replacing it with clean, weed-free top soil. Then seed or sod.

If you live in points east of the Rockies and particularly in southern Ontario, and your grass comes away easily, or can be rolled up almost like a rug in larger areas, chances are that it is a victim of white grubs. White grub is a collective name for the larvae of a number of scarab beetles, all with approximately the same life cycle. The damage they do tends to be more noticeable in mid- to late spring when grubs are large and feeding voraciously prior to early summer pupating. Often their presence can be confirmed without digging up a spadeful of soil since raccoons, skunks, and even foxes adore them as a succulent snack – which is the explanation for those holes all over your lawn. The adult beetles emerge in early to mid-summer to mate, whereafter the female lays her eggs and the whole cycle

repeats itself. Damage done by the small, newly-hatched grubs is rarely particularly noticeable. The best time to destroy these pests is when they are in this smaller stage. Do not wait until spring. The milkyspore disease is a natural control remedy that only works for Japanese beetles, which are found in small areas of south-central Ontario. All other white grubs and their adult beetles are immune to milkyspore and the only effective control for these pests is the chemical route, carbaryl (sevin).

Another cause of dead grass, particularly in British Columbia, Nova Scotia and south-central Ontario, is leatherjackets, the colloquial name for the larvae of the European crane fly. These larvae look like small, dirty-grey spindles and they have extremely tough skins, hence the name. The adult is common in late summer and early fall, and is similar in appearance to an enormous mosquito, although it does not bite or suck blood. Leatherjacket damage occurs in mid-to late spring only. Attacks must be confirmed by lifting out a spadeful of soil and sifting it carefully. Leatherjacket larvae are difficult to see and easily overlooked. Again, chemicals offer the only hope of control; leatherjackets are very susceptible to diazinon.

If your lawn damage occurs in midsummer, if the grass commences to die back in large irregular patches, particularly from flower borders or path edges, then your problem (except if your live in British Columbia) will almost certainly be chinch bug. This gregarious insect, both in its juvenile and adult stages, sucks the juices from the crowns of the grass plant. Chinch bugs multiply only when the temperatures are high, and rarely before the end of July, though they last to early September. Again, carbaryl (sevin) gives excellent control, although others claim insecticidal soap, a natural pesticide, is also effective.

There are other lawn pests which can cause damage but very rarely on the kind of scale of the four described above. In case of doubt, consult with provincial horticultural turfgrass experts or community colleges offering greens keeper courses. It is not often that garden centres have anyone on staff who is qualified to diagnose the more obscure turf problems. When finished reading this chapter, please also peruse that covering pathogens. Note, while the most serious pests require the use of chemical controls, most others do not. Those that do, require treatment to be applied at only particular times of the year. Some garden centre staff, as well as other retailers, seem to be under the impression that every lawn problem requires the purchase of something for its elimination. Given the potency of regulation pesticides permitted to be sold, it is odd that so little regulation is required, particularly as other less dangerous products are subject to much more careful legal control.

A lawn overrun with weeds may require selective herbicides for control of the broad leaf plants, and pre-emergence herbicides for crabgrass. It is equally possible, if you have time and physical ability, to remove the weeds by hand. Although, you may decide the chemical route to weed control is worth investigating after you've paid the chiropractor yet another visit. Prior to investing in lawn care chemicals, make sure you aerate and dethatch your lawn. Both of these procedures will require going all out, and using rented power equipment.

Aerators cut or punch a series of holes all over the lawn to relieve the inevitable compacting that comes from years of use. Aeration allows water and its dissolved mineral nutrients to percolate down through the root zone, in addition to allowing air to penetrate. Many people often overlook the importance of air, but the ne plus ultra of soils consists of some fifty percent solids, twenty-five percent water, and an equal percentage of air. The

> *If the grass is greener on the other side of the fence, ask your neighbour what fertilizer he uses.*
> Venerable gardening adage

so-called potting soils rarely achieve this mixture, and it is necessary to use "professional" or "soil-less" mixes, or "growing mediums" before such nirvana can occur.

Thatch is the layer of dead grass which exists under somewhat acidic conditions. Thatch may be caused by the natural soil acidity, or by the overuse of artificial fertilizers. Some claim that reliance upon liquid nutrient applications encourages its spread. The thatch layer is a marvelous nursery for a wide assortment of pests and diseases, many of which are rarely seen in its absence. Thatch also tends to choke grass growth while (as might be presumed from the name) forming an impermeable layer through which water and air cannot penetrate. Dethatchers, sometimes known in the trade as "vertical mowers," remove this buildup mechanically, and it is extraordinary just what quantity can emerge from even a small lawn, so be prepared for cheerful inquiries as to how your hay business is coming along. Thatch debris can be mixed with other organic waste and composted. Remember, any good cultural programme should eliminate thatching trouble in future seasons. Minor buildups may be removed with a rake. Spreading granulated horticultural lime will adjust the acidity upwards and also help release nutrients while improving the soil structure. Do not apply lime simultaneously with fertilizer as the two do not mix well together.

Okay, you are ready to conduct chemical warfare. A sprayer is not only unnecessary, on smaller lawns it may prove downright dangerous. One of the most common forms of damage to garden plants is accidental spray drift from selective herbicides. The smaller the area being sprayed, the more difficult to prevent such damage. The ubiquitous cheap green plastic watering can with its white nozzle is the answer. Mark "Danger - Herbicides" clearly in large letters on the side and use the can for nothing else, as removing every last trace of herbicide is extremely difficult. Use hose-end sprayers for larger lawns. Alternatively, some lawn weed control sprays come in a pre-mixed form with a hose-end sprayer built into the container – Wilsons is an example. Hose and sprayers are best used under very calm conditions, which often occur around dusk. As a courtesy to others, be sure you post signs (available at garden centres) that you have treated your front lawn with chemical controls. These have an almost instantaneous side effect insofar as they reduce the damage caused by dogs. Who said the neighbourhood pooches can't read?

Sometimes using one of the "weed-and-feed" granulated herbicides and fertilizers combined kills two birds with one stone, as it were. If the time of year is right for feeding, then by all means proceed, although most weed-and-feeds require that the weather remain dry for at least twenty-four hours following application. Crabgrass, on the other hand, is more easily controlled by spreading a pre-emergence herbicide to zap its seeds as they attempt to germinate. (This occurs about the same time as your forsythia bushes burst into their beautiful annual display of yellow.) The combined herbicide and fertilizer must be applied slightly before that time. This herbicide should be used only if you have professional confirmation of crabgrass which has seeded itself the previous late summer.

You've practiced proper mowing, irrigation, fertilization, aeration, dethatching, weeding, and pest control with all the zeal of a new convert to the latest diet. Yet the bare spots remain. Professional sportsfield supervisors often use an additional practice known as overseeding on an annual basis. Overseeding, as you might expect, involves scattering grass seed evenly across the playing field, and its perimeter, to thicken up the sod. Garden centres have caught on to this phrase and use it to sell much more seed than they might otherwise. Eager homeowners rush home to begin overseeding their lawns like so many suburban Ralph Waldo Emersons. Note, though, that Emerson was a philosopher and writer. His practical knowledge of lawn cultivation was nil. He even shied away from weeding his beans and the crop consequently failed.

Invest in a quality seed mix suitable for sun or shade, depending upon your lawn's circumstances. Remember that if the lawn receives less than six hours sun a day, it is a semi-shaded area. If it receives less than two hours of sun daily, it is in complete shade. So your lawn is half sun and half shade? You will need to choose a shade seed blend, because like many garden plants, seeds for shade grow well in shade and also in sun. The reverse, incidentally, does not hold equally true. Select a gravel rake and cultivate the entire surface vigorously prior to seeding. First rake from east to west, then do the same from north to south. Keep all other family members away from the area, because you are creating a properly worked-up seed bed and do not want it trampled down. Use a hand-held fertilizer spreader to distribute seed evenly over the entire lawn.

It is now essential to ensure that the grass seed comes in good contact with the soil. You can facilitate this by pressing the seed down lightly. On small lawns, this may be done by shuffling around the area with your feet. Your neighbours may have become sufficiently alarmed by your previously exhibited behaviour, like when you crawled over your lawn grubbing out weeds, so you may wish to wait until after nightfall to undertake this shuffle contact routine. Larger areas will require the use of a lawn roller twelve percent (one-eighth) filled with water. You can probably rent one, but if you do, make sure before you leave the rental yard that the plug in the hole through which you insert the water hose is removable and not rusted.

Grass seed takes up to a month to germinate completely and it must never dry out during that time. This means you should water very lightly by hand each and every day. Another alternative is to use a fine mist hose. Do not use an ordinary lawn sprinkler, as the force it generates will wash away the seed. Optimum time for overseeding is late in summer or very early fall, although this procedure is more popularly carried out in spring. By early summer, it is usually too late in all but the coolest and moistest parts of our northern regions to rely upon reestablishment.

What about the birds? Well, most don't eat grass seed. Those that do usually have better things to do, particularly at this time of year. But what the heck, if you are worried, sow an extra ten percent for the birds or keep your bird feeder filled to distract them. Best of all, forget the birds and concentrate on encouraging other kinds of phlox.

Does this sound like too much trouble? You might be right: it is largely a matter of personal opinion. Cheaper and less work to install are what we cheerfully call in the professional horticul-tural world "alternate ground covers." Chapter 9 provides an in-depth look at these plants col-lectively, and as individual species. Work and preparation for ground covers is exactly the same as that required for lawns. Sod may cost well over $2 a square yard, but most of the popular perennial alternative ground covers are planted at thirty centimetre (twelve inch) centres: in other words it takes nine ground cover plants to fill a square yard and they are a trifle more expensive than sod or seed. Ground covers will require as

much watering and weekly weeding as lawns do, along with fertilizing, pest and disease control, mulching, and other gardening activities. And they may not "establish" themselves or, in plain English, grow.

Another alternative is the professional residential lawn care company. You may wish to opt for the mowing and trimming yourself, but leave weed control and fertilization to professionals. If your pocket is deeper and your time in demand, you can pay to have a garden maintenance contractor take care of everything. Or you can call in the professionals to get your lawn into shape, then dismiss them and take over yourself. Having someone come in every week to take care of your lawn problems is like eating peanuts. It's addictive.

Physiological Disorders and Pathogens

Open spaces! Trees, leaves, bugs! Get me off this place, get me off!

Oscar Levant visiting Alexander Woolcott's island vacation home

The expression, "an ounce of prevention is worth a pound of cure," is as true for lawns as it is anything else. Just as human health suffers under unsanitary conditions and poor diet, a lawn's health will deteriorate rapidly when it is not properly maintained at the best height, watered, fed, aerated, and kept free of weeds and debris.

Prevention cannot be emphasized too much. When a lawn fails to receive reasonable care, it becomes target uno numero for every pest and disease in the neighbourhood. So the principal pathogen control methods are simply good cultural practices. These are:

- mowing to four to five centimetres (two inches) except for the final cut of the season
- applying a one centimetre (half-inch) of water every three days unless there is a heavy, sustained rainfall
- aerating in late spring and again in fall
- fertilizing in late spring and again in late summer or early fall
- raking clear of fallen tree and shrub leaves in the fall
- removing any thatch build-up

Common Physiological Disorders

Most lawn problems are caused by lack of care. We cannot emphasize this fact enough. It is only human nature to blame sick lawns on some exotic, uncontrollable cause. Turf grass care professionals and horticultural consultants quickly learn tact when their services are called upon. The simple fact is that the great majority of lawn disorders they encounter are not caused by pests or even diseases, but by deficiencies of culture.

The uncultured lawn, as elsewhere in life, attracts parasites. The first defense is a good offense: mow, water, fertilize, and aerate properly. You pride yourself on living a healthy life style, give your grass a chance to do the same.

Browning

Primary causes of browning are poor or nonexistent irrigation, and mowing too short – a condition turf fanciers call "scalping." Another cause is constant foot traffic immediately following winter. Foot traffic compacts the snow into ice and prevents air from penetrating the soil. Back yard flooding for skating rinks or ice hockey plays havoc with the underlying lawn and weeds will move rapidly into the poor suffering sod.

Burns

Lawn burns are caused primarily by careless handling and spreading of fertilizers, both chemical- and natural-based. Always fill a fertilizer spreader away from the lawn. Double check first to see that the lever which opens and closes the aperture at the base of the hopper is in the closed position. You will not obtain satisfactory results spreading fertilizer by hand.

Burning can also be caused by attempts to refuel gas lawn mowers while standing on the grass. Refuel your mower on the driveway or patio, but be aware that, even then, some surfaces can also be damaged or stained by gasoline and oil. Unilock distributes a product to clean unilock pavers and, although they understandably make no claims for other similar surfaces, you may wish to try this cleaner on any potential gas or oil stains you may make. Contact any dealer in your area or telephone 905-453-1438, fax 905-846-9236.

Grass growing under trees or utility wires – where birds regularly perch or roost – may also suffer burning from bird droppings which are extremely acidic. The same problem occurs under bird feeders located on or over your lawn. Move feeders to a location over a patio or deck where it will also be easier to sweep up the spilt husks and seeds before they, too, smother the grass. The commercial repellent "Rapel" has been claimed to be effective against birds without harming them. Commercial pest control firms can recommend other humane solutions. Dog urine and excrement also cause burns.

Smothering

Poor grass growth in spring is frequently caused by failure to rake up fallen leaves the previous fall. These smother the grass during the winter, as they mat down into a wet, obscene mass which prevents air penetration. If the leaves had been shredded (with the mulching attachment on your mower) they would have made excellent mulch for perennials, bulbs, and other tender garden plants. Raking them unshredded onto flower beds, however, causes the same problems as on lawns.

Compacting

Clay soils are especially prone to compaction. Frequent use – and what else are lawns for? – results in a solid surface through which air and water, with its accompanying nutrients, cannot easily penetrate. Consequently, lawn grass growth is poor. Compacted areas are also the favoured site of many weeds – crabgrass in particular. Additional watering and fertilizer will simply run off unless a regular aeration programme is undertaken.

Principal pathogenic problems with lawns are:
(not necessarily in order of importance)
- white grubs
- dogs
- chinch bugs
- leatherjackets

These four elements prove a law known as Murphy's Constant: "Matter will be damaged in direct proportion to its value." A healthy lawn can withstand surprising amounts of damage by any of these pests and recover well. Minor infestations may not even be apparent.

The minor pests comprise another group familiar to grounds keepers. At least these creatures remain minor until experts write them up in the literature and, suddenly, voila, everybody's lawn is seemingly under siege. Remember the European crane fly of Ontario in 1998?

Currently, known minor pests include:
- bluegrass billbug
- sod webworm
- turfgrass scale

Ants, millipedes, wireworms, grasshoppers and crickets, moles, groundhogs, earwigs, woodlice, dog ticks and fleas may also be regarded as occasional problems in the lawn pest department. Ants,

Natural Controls for Ants
- *Soda and vinegar poured onto the ant heaps*
- *Borax and molasses mixed and set out as baits*

despite recent favourable reviews, can also be pests in several ways. Some form ant hills in the lawn with devastating results when the mower blade, revolving at some three hundred and twenty-two kilometres (two hundred miles) per hour, comes into contact. Ants also encourage aphids, or plant lice, which are attracted by their sweet excrement. Have you ever parked your car under a large deciduous tree in the summer, and returned a few hours later to find the top sticky? The local aphid population has been dumping excrement on your vehicle from on high. Notice ants running up the tree trunk? They are protecting and encouraging the local aphid population. Isn't it educational what you can learn from gardening?

Millipedes eat grass seedlings. Keen pathologists tell us that millipedes have only about one hundred legs, not one thousand, two pairs to each body segment (which are grey to black in colour). When exposed, millipedes usually coil up like an old-fashioned watch spring. Centipedes on the other hand are good guys – predators that devour many other pests. Centipedes are usually brownish, with about twenty pairs of legs, one to each body segment. As a Victorian Lady wrote:

> *The centipede was happy quite,*
> *Until the Toad in Fun*
> *Said, "Pray, which leg moves before which?"*
> *And worked her mind into such a pitch,*
> *She lay distracted in the ditch*
> *Considering how to run*
> Mrs. Edmund Craster, 1874

Wireworms, the larvae of click beetles, are usually not a problem in established

---

Chemical Control of Pests and Diseases

This short list is a brief synopsis only. Please refer to concise directions in this chapter and on the pesticide container label.

Carbaryl (Sevin)
Bluegrass billbug
Chinch bug
White grub
Sod webworm

Diazinon
Leatherjacket

Benomyl
Dollar spot

Chlorothalonil
Dollar spot
Pink patch
Red thread

urban gardens, but they may well be one in suburban and rural areas, which were only recently open farmers' fields. Grasshoppers and crickets have been reported from time to time as causing some lawn destruction, particularly on the Prairies. Earwigs feast on flowers and should never, ever be mentioned in front of keen rose, dahlia, or chrysanthemum fanciers when there are also children present. Woodlice and billbugs, small armored primitive creatures more closely related to lobster and shrimp than anything else, may also attack seedlings, albeit rarely; these creatures should also be welcomed for their ability to break down organic debris.

Ticks, in gardens at least, are essentially a rural problem and they usually only occur in the longer, rough areas of grass on larger properties. Ticks can transmit a number of serious diseases to humans as, of course, can fleas. Both these pests are controlled quite easily with carbaryl (sevin) or diazinon. These are also effective against most of the other minor pests mentioned above. Chloropyrifos kills ticks only; malathion, fleas.

Skunks and raccoons can be a bother, particularly when blame must be allotted for holes suddenly appearing overnight in the turf. These animals are digging for white grubs. Remove that problem and holes-in-the-lawn is no longer a mysterious phenomenon. Moles will also be dissuaded from pursuing their nefarious nocturnal perambulations in search of the same. A cautionary note, moles are usually a problem of rural lawns or of urbanites fortunate enough to back onto a ravine or similar natural area.

Groundhogs can be found in somewhat the same situations. Although not attracted to the bugs within the lawn, they flock to the succulent vegetables nearby and sometimes even the ornamental plants. Some urban areas have laws making it an offense to interfere with the local groundhogs.

Pests

Lawn Pest Control Summary			
Pest	Time of Most Damage	Cultural Control	Chemical Control
Bluegrass Billbug	mid-summer	fescues, ryegrasses are resistant	carbaryl
Chinch Bug	mid- to late summer	heavy watering; avoid over fertilization	carbaryl
Dog	early spring	cayenne or chili pepper; block with fences, hedges	Rapel
Leatherjacket	spring	starling, natural parasite	diazinon
Sod Webworm	early to midsummer	tall, fine fescues resistant	carabryl
Turfgrass Scale	early summer	powerful hosing	none recommended
White Grub	spring	relished by many animals such as skunks, raccoons	carbaryl

---

Bluegrass Billbug *(Sphenophorus patvulus)*

CULTURAL CONTROLS: perennial ryegrass, fine fescue and tall fescue all resist feeding

CHEMICAL CONTROLS: carbaryl (sevin) may give some control

The larvae feast in mid-summer, severing the grass blades at ground level while sheltering inside the stems. The billbug's favourite food is Kentucky bluegrass, and it leaves brown patches upon feeding. Its habit of sheltering inside grass stems, where it is protected from the spray of choice – carbaryl (sevin) – makes it difficult to control completely. The larvae turn into adults by late summer, and move out of lawns into over-winter locations (those especially favoured are areas where the grass meets walkways, poorly weeded beds and leaf litter).

The billbug was not recorded as a lawn pest until 1967 when it suddenly emerged in upstate New York to devastate lawns without warning. Pathologists have postulated that the use of many chemicals on other more familiar lawn pests destroyed natural billbug predators, allowing it to multiply uncontrolled. Spraying with carbaryl (sevin) late spring is the best method of controlling adults before they mate and the female lays her eggs.

Dog *(Canis familiaris)*

CULTURAL CONTROLS: cayenne or chili pepper; fences; hedges, especially those of rose

CHEMICAL CONTROLS: "Rapel"

Natural Sprays

• *Many home-made formulations are recommended for use in the garden.*

• *If sufficient amounts of garlic are used, they are guaranteed to work.*

• *No gardener having used garlic spray has ever been attacked by a vampire while gardening.*

• *Garlic and hot pepper are also recommended as a spray. First reduce them to a pulp in a kitchen blender, then strain through coffee filter paper to remove fibre as it will block the sprayer nozzle.*

Dogs must be classed as a major lawn pest. Their feces are not only objectionable and unpleasant to clean from a hot lawn mower, but they are likely to contain roundworms. Few dogs allowed to run loose are free from these intestinal parasites which are also highly likely to be passed on to any children playing on the contaminated grass.

Canine urine is also a severe menace. It permanently pollutes the soil to such an extent that the grass dies. Damage is particularly noticeable following the melting of snow in the spring and thawing of the ground underneath. Larger dogs are a menace throughout the season. Smaller dogs, offering less exuberant contributions, may have their effects reduced by rains and irrigation. One of the very few dog repellents which appears to be effective is "Rapel," or Denatonium saccharide, developed by Atomergic Corp. It is claimed to be the bitterest substance in the world, and labeled "vile" by its inventor. Rapel is sold commercially as an animal repellent against dogs as well as raccoons, skunks, cats, and other mammals. It appears to remain effective for several weeks, its exact effectiveness duration dependent upon location, precipitation, and temperature.

European Crane Fly - Leatherjacket *(Tipulidae paludos)*

CULTURAL CONTROLS: A Tachanid parasite *Siphona geniculata;* starlings
CHEMICAL CONTROLS: diazinon

The leatherjacket was considered a serious pest only in southwestern British Columbia and the adjoining parts of Washington State up until 1998 (although it made its North American debut in Cape Breton, Nova Scotia in 1955, where it is believed to have landed in the discarded soil which was formerly a ship's ballast). By 1966, it had arrived in Blair, Washington. There were several reports of leatherjacket damage in Ontario in 1997, and these escalated the following year. At the time of writing, it is unknown whether leatherjackets will persist or whether, hopefully, they will succumb to more vigorous winters. According to entomologists, there are over a thousand species of crane fly native to North America, but so far only this wretched European species is a pest.

The leatherjacket is a dirty grey colour, spindle-shaped and feeds on both the roots and crowns of grass. It lives up to its name by having a hide as tough as a politician's. Stamping on leatherjackets is useless. These pests can be cut in two with spade or other implement. The pests' eating frenzy commences in early spring and lasts until mid-summer. Adults emerge in late summer and early fall, and resemble enormous mosquitoes. They do not bite. Following copulation, the female lays tiny black eggs which hatch a couple of weeks later.

A large number of starlings feeding on your lawn may be an indication of something amiss. Starlings are one of the very few birds that can handle the leatherjacket. Recently the minute parasitic Tachanid wasp was brought to the Vancouver area from its natural home in Germany and released to take up the fight against the local leatherjacket population. Although undoubtedly of some assistance, the Tachanid *Siphonia geniculata* wasp will never completely eliminate the problem. Fortunately, leatherjacket larvae are very sensitive to diazinon applied in late summer.

Hairy Chinch Bug *(Blissus leucopterus)*

CULTURAL CONTROLS: discouraged by watering; avoid over-fertilization;
                       claims have been made for insecticidal soap
CHEMICAL CONTROL: carbaryl (sevin)

Chinch Bug

The hairy chinch bug is a serious lawn pest in Ontario, Quebec, New Brunswick, Nova Scotia, New York, and the Northwestern states. It can, has, and does eliminate a lawn in under seventy-two hours thanks to its gregarious habits. Both the minute red nymphs, and the dark brown or black adults feed by sucking juices from lawn grasses, leaving rapidly expanding brown patches behind them. Look for chinch bugs in the zones of remaining green grass on the fringes of dead grass patches. Severe infestations and enormous numbers force some of these bugs out of the lawn onto surrounding walkways and driveways, resulting in damage to borders, beds, and shrubbery.

There is little that directly effects chinch bugs, although it does dislike regular watering especially during the opening stages of its early summer build up. Avoid creating too lush a lawn growth by over-fertilization. Water your lawn thoroughly forty-eight hours prior to applying carbaryl (sevin), and then desist from further watering for another twenty-four hours following the application.

Scarab Beetles - White Grub
Black Turfgrass Ataenius, *(A. spretulus)*
June Beetle, *(Phyllophaga* spp.)
Japanese Beetle, *(Popillia japonica)*
European Chafer, *(Rhizotrogus majalis)*

CULTURAL CONTROLS: Japanese Beetle: milkyspore disease; all are preyed
                       upon with gusto by skunks, raccoons, moles
                       and starlings
CHEMICAL CONTROLS: carbaryl (sevin)

All these are pests of northeastern America, and especially southern Ontario. The June beetle and European chafer swarm in late spring and very early summer, depending upon temperature. The black turf ataenius is a problem around the Great Lakes where there may be two generations a year. Japanese beetle has been reported in the same areas, from locations with sandy soils in the Niagara Peninsula, and around Hamilton, Burlington and Ancaster. June beetles are common throughout the northeastern region. They have a three-year life cycle. The European chafer prefers the relatively milder climates of the northeast – mid-Atlantic. All of these major pests cause almost identical damage in the larval stage, and gardeners lump them together under the heading of abominable white grubs. Professional entomologists confirm

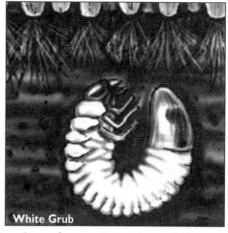

White Grub

individual species identification of the various larvae by examining the anal slot, which is a different shape for each.

Sod Webworm *(Family: Acrolopphidae)*

CULTURAL CONTROLS:	both tall and fine fescues tend to be more resistant as does perennial ryegrass; claims have been made for both diatomaceous earth and insecticidal soap
CHEMICAL CONTROLS:	carbaryl (sevin) which must be watered in lightly

---

Small nondescript brownish moths flying out of your lawn in early to mid-summer are an indication that sod webworm larvae or caterpillars are chewing the roots and severing them from the crowns. Some gardeners refer to these creatures as "cutworms," a generic term for the soil residing caterpillars of an alarming number of moths. Sod webworm adults usually only fly by day, and only when disturbed, as when the gardener walks across the lawn. Peak feeding activity is during the early hours of night. Damage is usually greatest in late summer although these pests are present earlier in the season. Since they are also found in the soil, it is essential to lightly water the chemical choice, carbaryl (sevin), following application.

Sod Webworm

Sod webworms, from one damaging species to another, are found all across the continent. Many are home-grown Canadian natives. The form most common in Ontario, *Chrysoteachia topiaria*, commonly known as the cranberry girdler, attacks grasses, cranberries, and conifer seedlings. A native earwig in California eats the eggs of this pest, but regrettably, webworms are not to the taste of the imported European earwig, which is much more common in Canada.

Turfgrass Scale (Lecanopsis formicarium)

CULTURAL CONTROLS:	spray heavily with a forceful jet from the hose
CHEMICAL CONTROLS:	none recommended; normal control for chinch bug also affect this minor pest

---

You will find turfgrass scale in early summer when the tiny, bright red nymphs are noticed on light-coloured footwear while walking over the lawn, sometimes in sufficient numbers to cause pinkish-red stains. These pests are spread to fresh areas on the feet of people and pets as well as by wind and other means. Adults are pinkish, waxy creatures clinging to the stems, where they and the nymphs feed by sucking the juices. Turfgrass scale was first reported in 1984 from a variety of professional and amateur sources in Ontario. It does not as yet appear to be a serious problem, certainly not enough to warrant specific use of chemical

---

Here are ten tips for successful use of chemicals in lawn care:

1. Read the label before spraying every time.
2. Mix only the amount required for the application in exactly the ratio indicated on the label.
3. Spray or dust on a calm day; for sprays use as coarse a setting as possible and guide the nozzle close to the grass to prevent unnecessary spray drift. The calmest part of the day is often close to dusk.
4. Wear rubber gloves used only for that purpose when applying chemicals. Launder all clothing immediately afterwards.
5. Do not eat, drink, or smoke during chemical application or even immediately after, until you have showered.
6. Do not permit children, pets, or other adults into the garden while you are applying chemicals.
7. Dispose of empty containers safely – most municipalities now offer special facilities.
8. Should friends or neighbours wish to use the same pesticide, lend them the entire container. Never, ever pour a portion of your chemical into another container even if it is marked with the same name.
9. Store all chemicals in a frost-free, secure environment away from children and irresponsible persons.
10. Never apply chemicals where they may harm wildlife, including aquatic life. Bees are especially sensitive to many chemicals as are other beneficial insects. Not only is it irresponsible to poison bees, it is illegal.

pesticides. Apparently it is better known in Europe where, in Poland at least, it prefers to feed upon red fescue.

Okay, enough with the animal pests. What about diseases? Yes, the following occur in lawns of northern climes: dollar spot, fairy rings, helminthosporum leaf spot, necrotic leaf spot, pink patch, red thread, rust and snow moulds. Good cultural practices keep such disease pathogens from becoming a problem.

Lawn Disease Control Summary

Pest	Time of Most Damage	Cultural Control	Chemical Control
Dollar Spot	summer	remove clippings	benonyl chlorothalonil
Fairy Rings	spring and fall	proper maintenance	none
Leaf Spot Heiminthosporum	early and mid-summer	do not fertilize early spring; mow higher; irrigate a.m. only	none
Leaf Spot Necrotic	early and mid-summer	remove thatch and reduce fertilization; aerate	none
Pink Patch	early summer	remove thatch, clippings; cut low in late fall	chlorothalonil gives poor control
Red Thread	early summer	remove thatch, clippings; cut low in late fall	chlorothalonil gives poor control
Rust	summer and early fall	remove clippings, fertilize	none
Snow Moulds	very early spring	cut low late fall; spread snow; vigorous raking	none recommended

Disease

Dollar Spot *(Sclerotina homeocarpa)*
CULTURAL CONTROLS: fertilize; remove clippings from lawn following mowing
CHEMICAL CONTROLS: benomyl or chlorothalonil

This is a summer disease favoured by warm, wet weather. It is attracted to lawns low in nutrients, specifically nitrogen. Hour-glass shaped markings appear on grass blades in patches about the size of a U.S. silver dollar (hence the common name). These patches may merge in heavy infestations.

Feed in mid-to late spring and remove clippings from the lawn either by mounting the grass catcher on your mower or by raking after cutting. If you are using chemicals, never, ever apply benomyl on consecutive occasions; alternate with chlorothalonil. Following application of the latter, do not mow or water for at least twenty-four hours. Apply chemicals immediately following the first appearance of the disease.

Fairy Rings (*several species of Fungi in the class Basidiomycetes*)
CULTURAL CONTROLS: remove underlying debris; lime; frequent heavy
                                         watering, fertilization, aeration, raking
CHEMICAL CONTROLS: none

Fairy rings are particularly noticeable in spring and fall, when the weather tends to be wet and a ring of toadstools may emerge. These may not be actually poisonous, although mycologists, or fungi fanciers, like to say that there are two kinds of mushroom eaters: old ones and bold ones. The fungus usually makes its presence known by forming circles or partial circles of dark green, fast-growing grass. This is owing to an excess of nitrogen created by the pathogen. Sometimes, albeit rarely, things will become more serious and the fungus well secrete toxic compounds which kill the grass. Soil inside the ring may be depleted of nutrients, consequently turf growth will be poorer.

Although frequent and heavy irrigation and aeration combined with liming in spring and again in the fall may assist, removal of debris under your sod is usually recommended. Note that heavy irrigation can actually favour other disease pathogens such as Helminthosporum leaf spot. Many experts suggest applying extra fertilizer to offset the nutrient deficiency. Alternatively you can remove the sod, and sterilize the underlying soil with chemicals or steam. There is no guarantee that the spores will not return. Fairy rings are not unsightly, and unless you are a lawn fanatic, I suggest that living with them is the best advice.

> ## Fairy Rings
> •*Traditional folklore said fairy rings were caused by fairies dancing in a circle on the grass.*
> • *Destroying a fairy ring is said to be unlucky.*

Helminthosporum Leaf Spot (*Drechslara and Bipolaris* spp.)
CULTURAL CONTROLS: avoid early spring fertilizing; raise mowing height,
                                         irrigate in morning only
CHEMICAL CONTROLS: none

This mouthful of a "common" name can be blamed on pathologists. This pathogen's scientific name was Helminthosporum, but a few years later botonists changed their minds, reclassifying it into two, naturally with different nomenclatures. Many turf grass experts still know it as Helminthosporum. Correctly, these are a group of diseases which cause leaf spots and blights, plus the far more serious crown and root rots referred to most accurately as "melting-out."

Cool, moist springs followed by hot, dry, early summers encourage this disease and it will cause severe damage. Feeding in early spring results in the lush grass growth especially prone to attack. If your lawn suffers a rapid die back, raise the mowing height and only water your lawn early in the morning. Leaf spot is encouraged by close mowing, too much nitrogen and over-irrigation, coupled with poor drainage.

Necrotic Leaf Spot (Leptosphaeria korrae)

CULTURAL CONTROLS: remove the thatch; reduce fertilization; water deeply; aerate

CHEMICAL CONTROLS: none

This disease of early and mid-summer results in "frog eye" patches in the turf. These have a bright green centre surrounded by dead brown grass. This leaf spot is probably the most common patch disease affecting lawns, particularly in late spring and early summer. Its principal victims are Kentucky bluegrass and fine fescue. Its patches are less than thirty centimetres (twelve inches) from where the roots have been killed or severely damaged during the previous fall and current spring.

You can control this disease by preventing drought stress through adequate and correct watering, and the removal of excess thatch through aeration. Turf grass experts agree that over-fertilization can encourage this leaf spot disease, but some pathologists have recommended applying natural "organic" fertilizers or composts to increase the micro-organisms that can suppress this pathogen.

Pink Patch (Limonomyces roseipellis)

CULTURAL CONTROLS: cut short on last mowing of the season, removing the clippings; remove thatch and avoid early spring fertilizing

CHEMICAL CONTROLS: chlorothalonil gives poor control

This is a very similar disease to red thread (see below), but not as serious. It is found mainly in Ontario and Quebec where it forms brown patches which may combine to cover larger areas. Chlorothalonil, the officially recommended chemical solution, gives poor control. Pink patch is best combated by understanding the underlying reasons for its development, and using cultural practices to discourage its onset. Pink patch is encouraged by acid soils. Frequent, shallow watering, or cool, wet weather allow it to attack its favourite lawn hosts: fine fescue and perennial ryegrass.

Common or Trade Names of Insecticides and Fungicides and Chemical Names

Benolmyl	methyl-1-(butylcarbamoyl)-2-benzamidazole carbamate
Carbaryl (Sevin)	1-naphthyl methylcarbamate
Chlorothalonil	tetrachloro isophthalonitrile
Diazinon	0,(0-)diethyl o-(2-isopropryl-6-methly-4-pyrimidinyl

You will notice a pink mycelium which will spread slowly. Apply horticultural lime following the manufacturer's recommended rates to help correct acid soils. Give your lawn a deep watering every three days as necessary. Thatch removal and avoiding early spring fertilizer applications should reduce the problem to a minimum.

Red Thread (Laetissaria fuciformis)

CULTURAL CONTROLS:	remove thatch; avoid early spring feeding; cut very short on final mowing
CHEMICAL CONTROLS:	chlorothalonil gives poor results; no others recommended

---

Red thread is a disease principally of fine fescue and Kentucky bluegrass. It is encouraged by wet conditions in early summer. The pathogen is similar to grey snow mould, but has red thread-like growths at the top of the grass blades which causes them to stick together. Red thread forms patches up to twenty centimetres (eight inches) in diameter and it can kill the grass roots in severe infestations. Its spores can be carried over the summer in thatch, providing another good reason for frequent thatch removal, particularly in areas of the country where springs tend to be cool and wet. Red thread may reoccur in fall when similar conditions favour it – optimum temperatures being in the range of 15 to 20C (60 - 70F).

In addition to removing thatch build-up, try to avoid early spring fertilizer applications. These encourage lush, susceptible growth. Lower the blades of the lawn mower to make the final cut of the year only about one centimetre (one-half inch) high.

Care with Chemicals

There are no dangerous chemicals, only dangerous people using them. Chemicals should be the last resort in your lawn-care programme. Always check first to see if a cultural, non-chemical means is available to control pests, disease, and weeds, although some so-called "natural" sprays and dusts may pose as much of an ethical and environmental problem. Like most chemical pesticides, these are total, non-selective eradicants, officially known as "broad spectrum." They kill *everything* in the way of arthropods – bad guys and good guys alike. Since the bad guys form a minute proportion of all insects and their ilk, this is akin, as we might say in military parlance, to using a nuclear weapon to wipe out a single sniper. Some naturally-derived chemicals can also have appalling effects on other wildlife. Rotenone is deadly to all water life: used near ponds, streams, and other bodies of water, it will eliminate all the fish. In fact, that is exactly what the rain-forest aboriginals, where it originated as a liana, used it for – fish poison – charmingly known in technical terms as a piscicide.

Rust (Puccinia spp.)

CULTURAL CONTROLS:	remove clippings from lawn following mowing; fertilize
CHEMICAL CONTROLS:	none

You know you have a problem with this disease when rust-like spots appear on the leaf blades of (mainly) Kentucky bluegrass, tall fescue and perennial ryegrass in summer and early fall. The pathogen is easily spread, and is especially encouraged by heavy dews and warm days. It is more prevalent under shade conditions and where drought stress has been coupled with infertile soil. Rust spreads easily, clippings from any affected lawn should be collected in the grass catcher and disposed of in a properly constructed and maintained compost heap. Removing excess thatch, and maintaining an on-going fertilizer and irrigation programme will largely eliminate this threat.

Snow Moulds (Typhula spp. and Microdochium nivale)

CULTURAL CONTROLS:	cut short on the last mowing of the season; spread snow evenly over the lawn during winter, remove clippings from lawn; rake vigorously
CHEMICAL CONTROLS:	none recommended

Snow moulds are pinkish or greyish patches which occur as the snow melts in spring. This disease thrives under very cold, wet conditions, particularly in shaded areas. It is prevalent on lawns throughout the colder parts of the country. In spring, it favours those areas where the snow cover persists for ninety days or more. The optimum temperature range for its formation is 0 to 7 C (32 - 45 F). *M. nivale* is sometimes known specifically as pink snow mould, while *Typhula* is called grey snow mould.

Both are discouraged by reducing the height of the mower blades on the final cut of the season to leave only a half-inch. Remove all clippings. When clearing adjacent paths and driveways over winter, spread the snow evenly on the lawn and do not allow large piles to accumulate, as these will be slower to melt in spring. Cold water emerging from the base will create optimum temperatures for snow moulds. Chemical control is so poor that we cannot recommend it. Use a leaf rake vigorously to disturb the mycelium. This should offer sufficient control on home lawns.

A Rogue's Gallery of Weeds

Whole woods have been swept away to make room for a little grass and a few American weeds.   Sir William Chambers, *Dissertation on Ornamental Gardening (1772)*

There are approximately three hundred plants in Canada that are classified as weeds. A weed may be defined as "any plant growing where it isn't wanted." This means that anything growing in the lawn, other than the desired species of grasses – even other grasses, can be considered a weed. To add insult to injury, almost all our weeds come from other continents, many from Europe, some from Asia and even an adventuresome few from Africa and South America. Did you know there were aliens at the bottom of your garden? Botanists, whose humour is sometimes completely resistible, label plants which have established themselves away from their geographical origins as "aliens." And that is exactly what they remain – alien and outcast from your lawn.

Fortunately only a few weeds represent any serious problem. Almost all the species in the following rogue's gallery of weeds may be controlled by normal cultural methods. It is important to realize – and admit to oneself – that weed problems in lawns are almost invariably caused by poor maintenance. By mowing your lawn to the correct height, watering regularly and thoroughly, and conducting a regular fertilizer programme, you can ensure most aliens' visits are brief ones. In recent years it has also been proven that aeration will make a considerable difference.

Perhaps, though, you have recently purchased your property, and your new lawn has had a total lack of maintenance. Don't panic. Even lawns consisting of as much as sixty percent weed are recoverable, although you may be required to use selective herbicides or call in a lawn-care company to do the job for you. With a lawn composition of sixty percent of weed or greater, it is suggested that you turn to Chapter 3 for information on establishing a new law.

You don't like using chemicals? You are absolutely right. You will now need to mow your lawn so as to leave at least five centimetres (two inches) of grass for almost the entire season. And never remove more than a quarter to a third of the total length of the grass blades at any one time. Reduce the height of your lawn to just over one centimetre (one-half inch) on the final cut of the year. This will encourage the grasses to form a thick mat which will choke out weed seeds in their infancy. Thick lawns rarely suffer from weed prob-

> *One year's seeding, nine year's weeding*
>
> old adage warning against allowing weeds to go to seed

lems. Make sure your lawn receives one centimetre (about one-half inch) of water every three days. The only natural substitute for this procedure is a heavy, prolonged rainfall. Feed your lawn with high-quality nutrients in late spring and again in fall using either a natural- or chemical-based fertilizer. Rent an aerator twice a year in spring and fall to improve the underlying soil. These necessary procedures are what lawn-care professionals call *cultural control*.

Back in 1870, British gardener, Charles Dudley Warner observed, "What a man needs in gardening is a cast-iron back, with a hinge in it." Medical science has produced 'Viagra' but alas, even today one can not buy or rent a stronger back. So it is down on one's knees to gouge, rip, and tear in a frenzy of frustration, wreaking havoc on the weeds in your lawn – those alien invaders – with sharp instruments. This exercise may not appeal to you, or perhaps there are small children or impressionable people watching. You may decide to resort to the chemical route.

Nobody advocates indiscriminate use of chemical herbicides. Provincial governments have strongly-worded laws to prevent commercial operators from doing just that. Furthermore, commercial operators must be licensed following stringent courses and written exams. It is the homeowner who is more likely to make errors especially if he or she seeks the advice of personnel in garden centres or other retail outlets which are not, strangely enough, covered by provincial legislation.

A lawn that is an eyesore to the neighbourhood and an infestation source can be recovered with the use of properly applied selective herbicides. These herbicides only take out (to use that military term) the bad guys, leaving the good guys unharmed. A pre-emergence herbicide kills seeds as they germinate. Exercise care with the mechanical spreader when applying in granulated form, so that you achieve an even application. Avoid any possible accidental treatment of surrounding vegetation, especially that of your neighbours. Liquid sprays can be even more tricky. Set the nozzle at the coarsest spray possible and choose a calm day. Better still, spray at dusk when there is usually the least breeze to spread unwanted drift. Hormone herbicidal damage may be cumulative in surrounding shrubs, and/or not show up for a year or more. Such damage can be confirmed by laboratory tests. And remember, much damage blamed upon careless spraying is caused by pathogens or other physiological disorders.

> *Rest for a while, yes, but there's weeding to be done.*
>
> Dutch proverb quoted by Douglas Chambers (1996)

Selective and pre-emergence herbicides give excellent control when applied at the correct times and proper rates. *It is then the homeowner's duty to*

Common or Trade Names of Herbicides and Chemical Names

Benulside (Betasan	0-0-disopropyl phosphorodithioate S-ester with n-(2-mercapttoethyl) benzenesulphonamide
Chloramben	3-amino-2,4-dichlorobenzoic acid
Dicamba	3,6-dichloro-o-anisic acid
EPTC	S-ethyldipropylthiocarbamate
MCPA	[(4-chloro-o-tolyl)oxy]acetic acid
Mecoprop	20[(4-chloro-o-toly)oxy]propoinic acid
Siduron (Tupersan)	1-(2-mehtylcyclohexyl)-3-phenylurea
2,4-D	(2,4-dichlorophenoxy)acetic acid

ensure that these herbicides need never, ever have to be used again. Most commercial lawn-care operators are so confident of their abilities that they offer written guarantees for weed elimination. If you do not feel up to this exercise yourself, perhaps it is time to call one. Many provinces have a professional horticultural trade association, Landscape Ontario is the largest. Check and see if the operator of your choice is a member of such an organization. They are rarely reluctant to divulge this information.

The following descriptions of individual weeds and their controls have been broken down into two major sections. The first lists the common name in Canada, the botanical name, and alternate names, if any. Readers seeking a concise and brief cultural method of chemical herbicides to control weeds find it in this section. The second section is of interest to those readers requiring a more detailed explanation, coupled with a little historical background and general information to amuse and entertain. Mention of every weed that might turn up in a Canadian lawn is impossible. Apart from the over three-hundred weed species we mentioned at the opening of this chapter, almost any cultivated plant can become one. Ask any gardener attempting to remove goutweed or bugleflower from his or her lawn!

Broad-leafed Weeds

Common Ragweed (Ambrosia artemisiifolia)

CULTURAL CONTROLS:	hand pull; correct mowing, irrigation, fertilization and aeration
CHEMICAL CONTROLS:	2, 4-d; mecoprop; dicamba

Native Annual

It is surprising how few people recognize this annual weed, even those hay-fever sufferers for whom late summer is a miserable time. Ragweed is inconspicuous, and it is ragweed, not the more showy goldenrod *(Solidago canadensis)*, which cause allergies. (Although even official government publications have written otherwise.) Ragweed has finely divided leaves rather in the manner of Italian parsley, with spikes of greenish flowers. Sometimes not very noticeable in the lawn, it can reach over one metre (five feet) in height. A close cousin, the well-named, Great Ragweed, *A. trifida*, of field edges and vacant lands, can reach almost five metres (fifteen feet).

Ragweed produces a vast numbers of seeds, which are remarkably long-lived in the soil. Nevertheless, this plant is very easily controlled either culturally or by use of selective herbicides. Our Aboriginal predecessors found several medicinal uses for ragweed, including relief from the itch of insect bites and infections through the use of fresh leaves. An astringent infusion was helpful for fevers and stomach cramps.

English Daisy *(Bellis perennis)*

CULTURAL CONTROLS: hand digging; correct mowing, irrigation, fertilization and aeration

CHEMICAL CONTROLS: 2, 4-D

• *alien perennial from Europe, especially England*

English daisies are seen more often on either coast rather than inland, because coastal climates are closer to its pluvial motherland. These plants can also be found even in the hot, humid summers of southern Ontario, and unless eliminated, they can become a major pest even in better-tended lawns. 2,4-D works well when applied in late spring or early fall, but two or more treatments spaced over a few weeks may be required. Anyone faced with controlling this pest will be less than happy to learn that there are also ornamental biennial forms for the flower border. English cricket-players refer to a ball driven low over the grass as a "daisy cutter." It is not a term of endearment.

Shepherd's Purse *(Capsella burrsa-pastoris)*

CULTURAL CONTROLS: pull out by hand; correct mowing, irrigation, fertilization and aeration

CHEMICAL CONTROLS: 2,4-D

• *alien annual*

Many bush-survival books note that this plant is edible. If you have sufficient shepherd's purse present to make a meal, your lawn must require drastic action. This is a common weed of garden beds, and any poorly-maintained lawn may become infested. It has a flower spike, but the complete plant rarely exceeds thirty centimetres (one foot) in height. Small white flowers are followed by heart shaped green unripe seed pods. Use caution when handling the plant, because it is a member of the mustard family and the seeds have been known to cause blisters. Shepherd's purse seeds and foliage were formerly used to make a tea which would stop bleeding and, when drunk, acted as a diuretic. The plant was also valued for treating diarrhea.

Mouse-eared Chickweed *(Cerastium fontanum)*

CULTURAL CONTROLS: difficult to hand weed; correct mowing, irrigation, fertilization and aeration

CHEMICAL CONTROLS: mecoprop or dicamba; resistant to 2,4-D when used alone but not in mixtures

• *alien annual or perennial*

Chickweed delights in entangling itself in with the grass blades, making it hard to remove by hand. The leaves are mouse-eared, hairy, and are also found on the stems, where they become sticky to the touch. The flowers are small and white. Chickweed, a plant of sprawling habit, is a close relative of the familiar grey foliated snow-in-summer of dry banks and rockeries.

Canada Thistle *(Cirsium arvense)*

CULTURAL CONTROLS: use a sharp knife to cut off immediately below the crown; correct mowing

CHEMICAL CONTROLS: 2,4-D or dicamba

• *alien perennial from Europe*

Baptized by our American neighbours this plant is not a native of Canada at all. It comes from Europe and Asia where it is called creeping thistle. Canada thistle is a major pest wherever it occurs. Although it seldom attains much stature in lawns, under favourable circumstances it can form sturdy stems which lack the spines found all too thickly on the leaves. The plant is topped with pale purple flowers on stems that usually rise a metre (three feet) or more above the ground. Canada thistle sometimes reaches three metres (almost ten feet). Most livestock find it impossible to graze on these plants, and their spines can blind an unwary animal. Walking in bare feet or lying on the grass is a risky act when this weed is present in lawns even as a very low plant.

Canada thistle is a perennial. Its rootstock is predictably strong and resists removal by hand, even for those willing to brave the thorns. Chemical sprays of combined herbicides should be used in mid-to late spring, as soon as the first leaves are observed.

The Scottish thistle, national flower of Scotland, is

> *The Canadian Thistle,* Cirsium arvense, *is perhaps the best reason for the invention of chemicals for killing weeds.*
>
> Eugene N. Kozloff (1976)

Canada Thistle

a close relation – and it is interesting to note that no other country seems ever to have chosen such a physically damaging plant for such an honour. Although the stem fibres are said to make good emergency twine, even the English, who seem to find a use for every plant on earth, haven't been able to do anything else with the thistle.

Ox-eye Daisy *(Chrysanthemum leucanthemum)* aka Field Daisy, White Daisy

CULTURAL CONTROLS:	hand dig with sharp knife or hand trowel; correct mowing, irrigation, fertilization and especially aeration
CHEMICAL CONTROLS:	2,4-D (applied in spring); 2,4-D mixtures

• *alien perennial*

The ox-eye daisy, also known as the field or white daisy, is like ragweed, a member of the Compositae family, and was introduced from Europe. The flower has white petals surrounding a yellow centre. The stiff, dark green stalk rises ten or fifteen centimetres (4 to 6 inches) from a rosette of leaves similar in shape to that of the common cultivated chrysanthemums. The ox-eye daisy has a distinctive smell.

Ox-eye daisies were dedicated to the goddess, Artemis. In the sixteenth and seventeenth centuries, they were used as a tonic for curing coughs and colds, as well as for healing wounds

> ## Daisies
> • *In some parts of America, it is believed that feeding puppies daisies will keep them small.*
> • *Said to have been created from Mary Magdelene's tears.*
> • *French knights in medieval times wore them into battle.*
> • *Drink an infusion of daisies every day for 15 days to cure insanity.*

and nervous conditions. In comparatively modern times, these plants found their way into the American pharmaceutica. In England, ox-eye daisy was used to cure childhood diseases now prevented by inoculations.

Ox-eye daisy root is somewhat rhizomatous, which makes pulling or hoeing difficult. Chemical control is achieved with 2,4-D, either by itself or in combination with other herbicides. Best sprayed in the spring or fall.

Bindweed *(Convolvulus arvensis)*

CULTURAL CONTROLS:	correct mowing, irrigation, fertilization and aeration
CHEMICAL CONTROLS:	2,4-D (several applications commencing in late spring)

• *alien perennial*

This is a weed of neglected lawns. Like couch grass, it is known descriptively by English country gardeners as the devil's guts. Every last piece of bindweed must be removed from the ground or the plant will resprout. Weeding is no easy chore

Bindweed

as it may become deeply rooted.

Bindweed was used (as a whole plant) by early settlers, who hopefully introduced it accidentally, as a laxative. Today the root is certainly recognized as that. Aboriginal peoples adopted it as relief from spider bites.

Common Mallow *(Malva neglecta)* aka Cheeses

CULTURAL CONTROLS:　　dig out by hand; correct mowing, irrigation, fertilization and aeration

CHEMICAL CONTROLS:　　difficult to control chemically, although 2,4-D applied twice holds it back

• *alien annual, biennial or short-lived perennial*

The unusually alternate name of the common mallow was arrived at by the resemblance of its seed pods to a round cheese. The blooms on this sprawling plant may range from white through shades of pink to mauve. There are other, closely related species with a very similar appearance. Any common mallow can be difficult to eradicate, once established in an old, neglected lawn. Proper cultural procedures offer the best solution but may have to be augmented by hand weeding.

As one humourist notes, weeding is similar to praying in church – you are often on your knees for both, only the language is a bit different.

Beverages brewed from common mallow leaves have, for thousands of years, been known to soothe sores both external and internal. These plants are distributed virtually all over the world. Common mallow pollen has been discovered in a Neolithic grave from some 50,000 years ago. In modern China, the leaves are said to be used for thickening soups and stews.

Queen Anne's Lace *(Daucus carota)* aka Wild Carrot

CULTURAL CONTROLS:　　dig out by hand; correct mowing, irrigation, fertilization and aeration

CHEMICAL CONTROLS:　　2,4-D

• *alien, usually a biennial, but also an annual or short-lived perennial*

One legend has it that Queen Anne of England challenged her court ladies to make lace as fine as the flowers of this plant, hence the name. Queen Anne's lace is also known as wild carrot, as indeed it is, but it also resembles the poison hemlock, *Conium maculaatum*. (This is the same plant used by the Greeks to cure politically incorrect philosophers, and no relation to the noble Canadian evergreen tree, confusingly also called hemlock.)

Queen Anne's lace remains a pretty flower of vacant fields. In the neglected lawn it is unlikely to gain much stature and is easily controlled. The roots are white and woody.

Ground Ivy (Glechoma hederacea) aka Creeping Charlie

CULTURAL CONTROLS:	difficult to eradicate by hand; correct mowing, irrigation, fertilization and aeration
CHEMICAL CONTROLS:	2,4-D mixtures (resistant to 2,4-D on its own), dicamba

• *alien perennial*

Ground ivy, one of Canada's commonest lawn weeds, especially in shaded, damp areas, came here from Europe. Canadian lawn owners are less enthralled with ground ivy, which is not actually a true ivy, but a member of the mint family – confirmed by examining the plant's stems, which are square in cross-section. When crushed, the plant gives off a strong odour. Its stems sprawl over the ground, somewhat like a strawberry, and take root at each node. The roundish leaves are dark green and the flowers, as might be expected, distinctly mint-like and blue.

Ground Ivy

The Saxons used it to clear their beer, and it is still known in Great Britain as "alehoof." Europeans made a tea from its leaves which was used for relief of any disorder – from digestive problems to coughs to headaches. American painters of the nineteenth century believed the same infusion would protect them from lead poisoning, an ever-present hazard in those days.

Black Medick (Medicago lupulina)

CULTURAL CONTROLS:	correct mowing, irrigation, fertilization and, especially, aeration
CHEMICAL CONTROLS:	mecoprop; dicamba; 2,4-D only when young

• *alien annual, thrives in poorly fertilized lawns*

If your lawn is favoured by flocks of feeding house sparrows in late summer, it is this seed that they are likely to be feasting upon. Although often treated with some contempt, the house sparrow, like many other common species, offers great assistance to gardeners by destroying many weed seeds and pests. Black medick foliage is often mistaken for clover, to which it is related as a member of the large

Black Medick

legume family. The yellow flowers of this plant are, indeed, pea-like and the seeds that follow, black and (it is said) nutritious. Various survival books recommend black medick seeds as a tasty dish, although given the amount of seed needed to provide a square meal, one person would probably be too exhausted to eat the dish after collecting it.

This is another weed on which 2,4-D is not entirely effective. Apply dicamba or mecoprop, instead, in spring or very early summer if choosing the chemical route to control. Fall applications, after the seed has been shed, are a waste of time and money, and can cause unnecessary pollution.

Narrow-leafed Plantain *(Plantago lanceolata)* aka English Plantain

CULTURAL CONTROLS:　　dig out by hand; correct mowing, irrigation, fertilization and aeration

CHEMICAL CONTROLS:　　2,-4D, mecoprop; resistant to dicamba

• *alien annual*

This species, as its common name implies, has much narrower leaves than its better-known cousin, the broad-leafed plantain, *P. major*. The flower heads are also very different to anyone but a botanist. English plantains have wiry stems thirty centimetres (one foot) in height, topped with a blackish club from which white flowers emerge.

These plants appear mainly in neglected lawns, and are not usually as invasive as *P. major*. English plantain is reasonably easy to control culturally, with a little patience, because it is an annual. If the flower heads are not allowed to form, but mown continually, no seeds will be generated and the weed will die out after a single season.

Broad-leafed Plantain *(Plantago major)* aka Whiteman's Foot, Englishman's Foot

CULTURAL CONTROLS:　　dig out by hand; correct mowing, irrigation, fertilization and aeration

CHEMICAL CONTROLS:　　2,4-D; mecoprop; resistant to dicamba

• *alien annual or perennial*

The broad-leafed plantain was catalogued by the Roman naturalist, Pliny, and held to be a sacred herb by the Saxons. Its liquid extracts have been reportedly used by the Chinese, who have also used the stem and seeds for bird food and cosmetics. Its young leaves provide a good example of the dictum "if you can't beat 'em, eat 'em," as long as no spraying has taken place in the vicinity and your neighbours' dogs have not contributed any additional flavour. In folk medicine, these plants are

crushed or pulped and placed on stings, bites or burns, a substitute for the curled dock leaves *(Rumes crispus)*. The seed
pods of a closely-related species, grown commercially in
India, form the base for a well-known and mild commercial laxative.

Broad-leafed Plantain

Legend has it oft repeated that the common
name is derived from the plantains' habit of following Caucasian colonizers. Actually, however,
the scientific name, *Plantago*, is derived from *plan-
ta*, Latin for the sole of the foot, because the leaves
are broad and press closely to the ground – like
the sole of the foot.

Broad-leafed plantain is usually a perennial
and somewhat more difficult to control than its nar-
row-leafed relative. It can be dug out easily and is susceptible to eradication
through good cultural practices. Chemically, it is killed with ease by 2,4-D or
mecoprop, although resistant to dicamba.

Prostrate Knotweed (Polygonum aviculare)

CULTURAL CONTROLS: dig out by hand; correct mowing, irrigation, fertilization and aeration

CHEMICAL CONTROLS: dicamba or 2,4-D mixtures applied to young plants; older plants resistant

• *alien annual*

The prostrate portion of its common name describes this weed precisely. It is
further easily recognized by its pink-tipped flowers when in bloom. The scientific
name is derived from the Greek, *polys* and *gony*, or many kneed. In China this plant
is used medicinally to assist painful urination, treat gonorrhea, and cure roundworms. One could only wish this weed could find some similar uses in Canada.

Prostrate knotweed is another common colonizer of neglected lawns, especially
those which become compacted through lack of regular aeration. Caution should be
exercised when attempting to hand weed, as this plant snaps easily at its joints and
sections left behind will resprout. Chemically, dicamba gives excellent control but
prostrate knotweed has shown marked resistance to other selective herbicides,
although 2,4-D in mixtures is still effective.

Japanese Knotweed (Polygonum cuspidatum) aka Bamboo

CULTURAL CONTROLS: dig out by hand several times annually until eliminated; mowing will assist

CHEMICAL CONTROLS: none in lawns; resistant to all selective herbicides

• *alien perennial*

Anybody who has experienced this weed in his or her garden will find it difficult to believe it was originally introduced into this country as an ornamental from the Orient. Japanese knotweed can form enormous thickets, up to four metres (thirteen feet) tall, in river bottom lands. Its hollow, distinctly jointed stems, flecked with reddish purple, do indeed somewhat resemble bamboo. The stems die in late fall, although often remain standing until spring the following season, when new reddish shoots emerge.

Japanese knotweed spreads quickly, unless its underground rhizomes are dug out and destroyed. Do not compost them, until they have dried and shrivelled on a paved area for several days. Wilson's Poison Ivy & Brushwood Killer, with ammonium sulfamate, is a **total herbicide**, and the only chemical that can control this weed. It is not poisonous to animals and breaks down over a year or more. Some gardeners have also reported success with brushing the young knotweed leaves with this herbicide which is then said not to affect surrounding plants. It should be emphasized, however, that the herbicide is not licensed for such application.

Curled Dock *(Rumex crispus)* aka Yellow Dock

CULTURAL CONTROLS:	digging out with sharp knife or trowel; correct mowing, irrigation, fertilization and aeration
CHEMICAL CONTROLS:	2,4-D or dicamba applied spring or fall

• *alien perennial*

Curled dock gains its common name from the wavy or curled margins of its leaves. The botanical name *Rumex* derives from the traditional Roman name for the weed, which was well-known to them. The seed head is most distinctive, and can reach over one metre (three feet) high at times. When ripe, it is a glorious rusty red. A favourite abode for earwigs, curled dock is rarely a problem in well-established and maintained lawns. Since it yields with reasonable ease to digging out by hand, it rarely justifies herbicide use. Both 2,4-D and dicamba will give good control if necessary.

Curled dock has been used as an herb and for the relief of a wide range of medicinal complaints including skin problems, diarrhea, or "blood purification." It has been demonstrated that excess use of this plant can cause equally serious medical problems. One old folk remedy for the relief of itch caused by close encounters with stinging nettles is curled dock, and strangely enough, dock almost always seems to be found growing close to where nettles flourish.

Curled Dock

Purslane *(Portulaca oleracea)*

CULTURAL CONTROLS:	correct mowing, irrigation, fertilization
and aeration

CHEMICAL CONTROLS:	EPTC or chloramben or chlorthal-dimethyl
pre-emergence herbicides (last is also used for
crabgrass control)

• *alien annual*

Purslane, a prostrate, succulent weed, was once a sovereign cure for scurvy, a much relished salad herb, and pickled by the Dutch for winter consumption. It is reported to be extremely nutritious. A close relative of the exceedingly ornamental annual portulaca, purslane tolerates drought exceedingly well, may colonize skimpy, neglected lawns lacking proper irrigation. It is very rarely a problem in well-maintained lawns.

The early Romans called this weed *portulaca*. It was used in Europe for painful urination and is indeed a diuretic. North American Aboriginals used it on burns and for ear, head and stomach aches, after its introduction here by early settlers. Supposedly it is also a cure for irritation caused by the hairs of various caterpillars.

As an annual, Purslane is easily controlled if prevented from blooming by constant mowing or other cultivation. Hand weed with care as the stem snaps easily into segments, each of which will root again. Use herbicides in late spring only, as with most annual weeds. Pre-emergence herbicides may give control as well: chlorthaldimethyl is often found in granular crabgrass control, blended with fertilizer. Apply in spring before the forsythia blooms have completely opened.

Creeping Buttercup *(Ranunculus repens)*

CULTURAL CONTROLS:	correct mowing, irrigation, fertilization and
aeration

CHEMICAL CONTROLS:	2,4-D; MCPA; mecoprop

• *alien perennial from Europe and Asia*

Care should be exercised when pulling this weed by hand. The juice is acrid and was used by beggars in medieval Europe to raise suppurating sores and welts in a bid to appear more worthy of pity. For some undetermined reason this weed was known in England as rain poll.

> # Do You Like Butter?
> *English school children hold a buttercup flower under each other's chin.*
> *A yellow reflection on their skin, makes them believe they like butter.*
>
> # Buttercups
> *Formerly were hung in bags around the necks of lunatics to effect a cure.*

Heal-all *(Prunella vulgaris)* aka Self-heal

CULTURAL CONTROLS:	correct mowing, irrigation, fertilization and aeration
CHEMICAL CONTROLS:	mecoprop or dicamba mixtures with 2,4-D (resistant to 2,4-D alone)

• *alien perennial*

This is a low or creeping weed, a member of the Labiatae, or mint family, with the typical square stems of such plants. As might be expected, the flowers are a deep purple or violet.

Heal-all was used medicinally in Europe and by the colonists of North America for sore throats in particular, as well as fevers and diarrhea. It is also utilized in traditional Chinese medical practice for liver and kidney problems, among others.

Dandelion *(Taraxacum officinale)*

CULTURAL CONTROLS:	use sharp knife to severe taproot at least three inches below surface; correct mowing irrigation, fertilization and aeration
CHEMICAL CONTROLS:	2,4-D or 2,4-D mixtures

• *alien perennial from Europe, Asia*

Dandelion's botanical name is derived from Persian *talkh chakok*, or bitter herb; its common name is from the French, teeth of the lion, in reference to the leaf shape. In Newfoundland, these plants are called piss-a-beds because of their diuretic action. The young foliage is cultivated specifically for culinary purposes, but excess consumption may prove embarrassing.

There is vast literature on the various uses to which dandelions may be put. Its dried root can be ground up as a coffee substitute or used fresh as a tonic. Medicinally it has been traditionally used as a diuretic, as well as for problems of the elimination organs. One source claims the Scots obtained a dye for their tartans from dandelions.

Dandelion wine is very popular in rural England. But it was the Russians who succeeded in perhaps the most extraordinary use of the plant, when during the Second World War they produced rubber from a species native to the steppes.

Dandelions find it hard to become established when the grass is kept five centimetres (two inches) high, well-watered, and aerated frequently. Attempts

Dandelion

made to remove them with a knife or other implement require an insertion at least eight to ten centimetres (three to four inches) below the crown of the plant to severe the tap root. Even then it may be necessary to repeat the performance several times. Spot treating with selective herbicide is an alternative. Several companies market handy aerosols which include a foaming agent to mark which weeds have been treated.

> ## Dandelion Divination
> *The number of breathes it takes a young maiden to disperse all the seed from a dandelion head will tell her the number of years before marriage – or the number of children she will have.*

Chickweed *(Stellaria media)*

CULTURAL CONTROLS: pull out by hand; correct mowing, irrigation, fertilization and aeration

CHEMICAL CONTROLS: 2,4-D; mecoprop

• *alien annual or perennial*

Chickweed rarely grows much more than fifteen centimetres (six inches) tall. Its fresh green mound, which may migrate from garden beds, is all too well known. It is a particularly common weed of greenhouses in some areas, and may turn up alongside annuals or perennials brought in from retail outlets. Chickweed is particularly easy to control if hand pulled prior to seeding when behaving as an annual. It is primarily a problem of poorly cultured lawns.

Chickweed has been used in traditional medicine to relieve coughs, itches and inflammations. It is also claimed to benefit overweight persons when consumed. None of these assertions, however, have been proven by modern medical science.

White Clover *(Trifolium repens)*

CULTURAL CONTROLS: correct mowing, irrigation, fertilization and aeration

CHEMICAL CONTROLS: 2,4-D; mecoprop

• *alien perennial*

The intentional use of clover in lawns undoubtedly dates back to the bucolic days of the eighteenth century when the sweeping lawns of Ye Olde England were kept trimmed by cows. In the more recent past, grass seed sold for lawns was often mixed with that of clover on the peculiar grounds that it made for a better lawn. Not so. Lawns with clover are extremely slippery under most weather conditions, particularly so when the slightest bit moist. This hazard can result in serious injury from slipping on the slightest slope and perhaps even on level lawns. On a lesser but nonetheless annoying note, clover also stains clothing.

> ## Clover
> *In France, the superstitious believe clover grows best beneath a gallows where it feeds on the blood of the hanged.*

Fortunately, white clover and its close relative, red clover, both submit to normal lawn care. It may be necessary to resort to chemicals like 2,4-D or mecoprop to bring it under control initially. Clover is a legume and can compete on poorer soil and/or under drier, more adverse conditions than can lawn grass. Traditional medicine used an infusion of clover blooms to treat gout and rheumatism. Aboriginal people used clover leaves for relief from coughs and colds. The traditional Irish shamrock, or at least many of the pots of something sold as it on St. Patrick's Day, are nothing more than consecrations of clover whose seed has been especially selected because of its propensity for four leafed plants. Outside of Ireland, the shamrock is a four-leaf clover and reputedly a lucky charm. Whether you want clover growing in your lawn depends on your individual view point.

Purslane Speedwell (Veronica peregrina)

CULTURAL CONTROLS: difficult to eliminate by hand; correct mowing, irrigation, fertilization and aeration

CHEMICAL CONTROLS: 2,4-D mixtures with mecoprop and/or dicamba

• *alien annual*

Tiny white flowers shaped like snapdragons reveal this weed's family, which technically is Scrophulariaceae. Attempts at hand removal will prove extremely difficult because of the generous seeding habits of speedwells. This seems a little hard on St. Veronica, from whom these weeds take their name. There are several other very similar species which can also infest sod. Resorting to herbicides will still probably require several application.

> **Speedwell**
>
> *In 19th-century Yorkshire, England it was believed if a child picked speedwell flowers, his or her mother would die within the next twelve months.*

Narrow-leafed Weeds

Barnyard Grass (Echinochloa crusgalli)

CULTURAL CONTROLS: mow regularly to remove seed heads; carry on good cultural practices

CHEMICAL CONTROLS: pre-emergence herbicides (see crabgrass)

• *alien annual*

Barnyard grass is a coarse grass with a distinctive seed head, coloured dark green to dark purple, with large roundish seeds. It is frequently misidentified as quackgrass or annual blue grass, although it does not resemble either in the slightest way. Like most annual weeds, barnyard grass is easily controlled by preventing it from seeding, or adjusting the mower so that it removes seed heads before they ripen. Prevent any seeds from germinating and becoming established,

An English Lawn with Weeds

One early English expert, John Claudius Loudon, suggested in 1803 that the lawns at Scone Palace be left unmown. This would allow daisies, thyme, saxifrage and clover to become established in patches. Loudon is acclaimed as publisher of the first *Gardener's Magazine*. Both he and his wife were prolific and influential writers on horticultural subjects.

if they do find their way into your lawn by wind or other transport, by utilizing good cultural practices, particularly mowing to the correct length, watering, fertilization and aeration.

Quack Grass (Agropyron repens) aka Couch Grass, Scutch Grass, Twitch Grass, Witch Grass

CULTURAL CONTROLS: regular mowing to "behead" it, watering, fertilization

CHEMICAL CONTROL: none

• *alien perennial from Eurasia*

Quack grass is the politician of grasses. It spreads through incredibly tough and extensive rhizomes below the surface. Once these become mixed with regular turf grasses they are virtually impossible to remove by hand without destroying the sod. Cultural control take some years to achieve. Mowing is the most vital. Beheading the brute immediately after it protrudes above other grasses also helps. Fertilizing and, especially, watering will also assist. Interestingly, a close relative, *A. smithii*, is one of the principle components of short-grass prairies. Quack grass was known in herbal medicine as a diuretic and dewormer which explains why cats will often eat as an emetic. The rhizomes, when lightly roasted, are claimed to make a beverage equal to coffee.

Quack Grass

Orchard Grass (Dactylis glomerata)

CULTURAL CONTROLS: digging out clumps with a knife or trowel

CHEMICAL CONTROLS: none

• *alien perennial*

Orchard grass is a tufted grass with somewhat flattened seed heads that are quite distinctive. It is widely sown agriculturally in hay mixtures – thus an excellent reason never, ever to use hay as a mulch. Choose straw instead. If present in

Orchard Grass

modest amounts, orchard grass is a relatively simple matter to eradicate by hand; dig out the clumps using a bulb trowel or sharp knife. If this results in a hole, do *not* fill with fresh topsoil from the garden, as this will likely inoculate the lawn with more weeds. Use prepared, bagged potting soil for indoor plants instead. You can obtain this from garden centres and other retail outlets. Orchard grass will be discouraged from establishing itself with good cultural practices. If these seem to be excessive of time and money, note that severe infestations of this coarse grass can result in replacement of an entire lawn.

Crabgrass (Digitaria spp.)
Smooth Crabgrass (D. ischaeum)
Hairy Crabgrass (D. sanguinalis)

CULTURAL CONTROLS:	mowing grass high; collecting seed heads in mower's grass catcher
CHEMICAL CONTROLS:	pre-emergence herbicides (see text below)

• *native annual*

Spring advertising campaigns of garden centres in Ontario and Quebec almost invariably contain "specials" on crabgrass control fertilizers. These contain *pre-emergence herbicides* which zap seeds as they attempt to germinate. Notice the

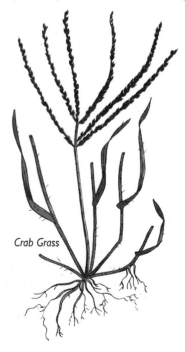

Crab Grass

word "seeds." Almost all of these remedies commonly sold kill *all* seeds for an extended time following application (most manufacturers note a minimum period of ten or twelve weeks). This means that reseeding after applying pre-emergence herbicides is an exercise in futility. The only pre-emergence herbicide that does not kill other seeds, including lawn grasses, is siduron (Tupersan). Pre-emergence herbicides do offer excellent control when applied *prior* to the forsythia coming into blossom, by which time the seed has germinated. Two other pre-emergence herbicides commonly used for crabgrass control are bensulide (Betasan) and chlorthaldimethyl. Follow the manufacturer's direction exactly, as in the use of all pesticides and herbicides.

Crabgrass adores hot, dry weather while most lawn grasses dislike such conditions. Crabgrass

> ## Clearing up the Moss Mysteries
>
> According to an article by Laurie Scott in *Landscape Trades* (June 1998), mosses are some of the oldest plants in the world and may lend themselves to shade gardening. Acknowledging that they prefer acid conditions, Ms. Scott suggests working peatmoss into alkaline soils, then adding rocks for additional interest. Moss clumps, she says, may be placed a foot apart and watered daily to encourage growth. The only maintenance required, once this occurs, is regular watering and weeding. A moss garden professionally installed in Toronto's High Park area uses a computerized drip irrigation system to mist the moss four or five times daily. Conifer needles which accumulate must be raked off carefully. Sorry, no leaf blowers here.

does not compete until midsummer if your lawn is kept properly watered and mown, and it will still not compete in late July through early September if these controls are maintained. Crabgrass infestation can be detected by the purple sheen which appears as the massed seed heads prepare to shed and lie dormant until the following spring. Once the crabgrass has seeded, being an annual, it dies. This results in large bare or sparse patches which may then be overseeded.

Spraying with post-emergence herbicides when the seed heads have ripened to a purple sheen is useless, as the crabgrass is about to die anyway.

Neither species of crabgrass is normally a problem of well-maintained lawns. Never cutting below five centimetres (two inches), conducting a reasonable fertilizer programme, using natural or chemical nutrient sources, irrigation, and aeration will eliminate potential problems before they commence. If you inherit a neglected lawn in late spring or summer and notice the seed heads emerging, mow with a grass catcher attached to catch cut heads. Ensure that these are composted properly or they may become a problem elsewhere later.

Squirreltail Grass (Hordeum jubatum) aka Foxtail Barley, Wild Barley
CULTURAL CONTROLS: dig out individual clumps
CHEMICAL CONTROLS: none
• *believed to be a native annual, biennial or perennial*

Not surprisingly, this grass has the appearance of cultivated barley. Squirreltail grass is sometimes planted as an ornamental. This is enough to make any good rancher lose his breakfast. Despite its graceful, arched heads, squirreltail grass spikes are so sharp that they can pierce the tongue of an unwary steer. It is regarded as a weed in the home lawn, but is more a problem of neglected or poorly maintained sod. A good lawn maintenance programme will usually eliminate squirreltail grass. In small quantities, it can be easily removed by hand using a bulb trowel or sharp knife. Fill in the resulting holes with pasteurized potting soil sold by the bag at the local garden centre or other retail outlet. This grass is resistant to all lawn selective herbicides.

Timothy *(Phleum pratense)*

CULTURAL CONTROLS:	dig out individual clumps
CHEMICAL CONTROLS:	none

• *alien perennial*

Timothy

An English farmer, Timothy Hanson, sang the praises of grass for use in pasture and durums in the early eighteenth century. Timothy was first recorded in North America slightly earlier by an acute New England observer, Jonathan Heard. It is not known whether this was an intentional or, as is more likely, an accidental introduction. Timothy is valuable hay grass and still widely planted agriculturally.

The Timothy seed head is a distinctive "foxtail" and unmistakable. Unfortunately, its wide use in the farming community has resulted in hay containing large amounts of Timothy seed. Thus hay makes unsuitable mulch. Since the same hay is fed to cattle, who have notoriously inefficient digestive systems, Timothy is also a frequent component of poorly composted manures. It is for this reason that the spreading of "composted" manure over lawns is not recommended.

Timothy grows in clumps rather than spreading by creeping root stocks or stolons. It may be dug out by hand when present in modest amounts. Normal cultural practices will discourage its initial arrival – and is by far the best method of elimination. There are no effective chemical controls for lawns.

Buttermilk Makes Better Moss

Want to encourage moss to grow on rocks or planters made of concrete, stone or metal? One old gardening "trick" is to paint these containers with buttermilk or yogurt. This will also encourage the growth of lichens and algae. If moss alone is required, whip some up in a blender together with yogurt or buttermilk, then apply to the surfaces where it is desired. Experts report that plain or flavoured yogurt may be used, according to your taste.

Chemical Weed Control				
This chart is a summarization only				
2,4-D	**Dicamba**	**Mecoprop**	**Ammonium Sulfamate***	**EPTC**
Common Ragweed	Common Ragweed	Common Ragweed	Japanese Knotweed	Purslane
English Daisy	Mouse-eared	Mouse-eared		
Shepherd's Purse	Chickweed	Chickweed		
Ox-eye Daisy	Canada Thistle	Black Medick		
Canada Thistle	Ground Ivy	Narrow-leafed		
Bindweeed	Black Medick	Plantain		
Queen Anne's Lace	Prostrate Knotweed	Broad-leafed		
Common Mallow	Heal-all	Plantain		
Narrow-leafed	Curled Dock	Heal-all		
Plantain	Purslane Speedwell	Creeping Buttercup		
Broad-leafed		Chickweed		
Plantain		White Clover		
Prostrate Knotweed		Purslane Speedwell		
Curled Dock				
Chickweed				
Dandelion			* *a total herbicide*	
White Clover				
Purslane				

Chloramben	**Chlorthal-dimethyl**	**MCPA**	**Bensulide (Betasan)**	**Siduron (Tupersan)**
Purslane	Purslane	Creeping Buttercup	Crabgrass	Crabgrass
	Crabgrass		Barnyard Grass	Barnyard Grass
	Barnyard Grass			

Simple Plants

Mosses *(botanically complex group - several invasive of lawns)*

CULTURAL CONTROLS: correct underlying problems e.g. shade, drainage, low fertility

CHEMICAL CONTROLS: none; lime may assist

• *most are native to Northern Temperate Zones*

Although the intentionally cultured moss gardens of Japan attract universal interest, we will assume that moss has achieved the status of an unwanted weed in most Canadian lawns. Managing a moss garden is not as easy as finding this weed over most of the country.

Mosses invade lawns only when poor cultural conditions for grasses or most other plants prevail. These conditions must be corrected, if possible, or at the least reduced to achieve successful control. This is frequently easier said than done in coastal British Columbia. Prune back trees and tall shrubs to allow for good air circulation and so that additional light reaches the sod. Commence a regular fertilizer programme to improve nutrient content of the soil, which may also be too acidic. Kentucky bluegrasses require a pH of around 6.5 while fescues tolerate lower levels and grow better in shade. Regular application of horticultural or garden granulated lime will greatly benefit moss-ridden lawns because it will raise the pH back up nearer to neutral. Apply very late in the season, after the final mowing in all areas except coastal British Columbia, or in March and April well before the first fertilizer is spread.

Equipment and Its Maintenance

I'm standing in a semicircle of maybe 500 people on a carpet of lush, sweet-smelling green-glinting grass, the kind that makes you want to get naked and roll on your back like a dog.

Dave Barry (1997)

The Cutting Edge
Reel Mowers

Spike Milligan, the British humourist, is unfortunately also manic-depressive. Excessive noise can result in an attack, even the sound of a motor mower. Who can not find sympathy with him? The real thing for sufferers like Spike, and the rest of us who overdose on decibels is the reel mower: a sharpened spiral of blades set around a central spindle activated by a pair of wheels when pushed. This gives rise to its alternate name "push mower," and as with any popular personality, these machines attract other names, often simply the "hand mower." Nonetheless, whatever name you call it, the mower's blades still operate against the bedplate with a scissor action, giving the best and most perfect cut invented for lawns.

Powered rotary mowers tend to rip rather than cut cleanly, especially when sharpened infrequently or not at all.

Rotary mower blades can be sharpened by hand. A reel mowers' cannot. Reel mower blades become somewhat dulled by the end of each season, with slight nicks from coming in contact with objects other than grass. They must be sharpened by a professional, who can be found

> *It is said the decibel level permitted in the leafblower is 70 dBA at a measurement distance of 15 metres. It turns out, this is just 3 dBA below an air compressor and a mere 13 dBA off that of a pneumatic pavement breaker.*

at the local hardware store. Consult your 'Yellow Pages' for the one nearest you. And don't wait until spring when everybody else has the same idea. Take your mower in to be sharpened immediately after the final cut of the year. West Coast gardeners can conveniently ignore this dictum: nothing ever seems to stop growing in that beautiful part of the country. Calgary residents remark enviously that people do not go to Victoria to retire – they go there to rust.

Not only do reel mowers offer the best cut, they are also environmentally friendly. The gentle whir of blades will not disturb even the most delicate of slumberers, nor choke the neighbourhood with noxious fumes.

When finished mowing, always clean off any cuttings and other debris from your mower. Wipe down all metal parts with an oil cloth, and store the machine in a dry, protected area. An occasional application of lubricating oil to the bearings will ensure a longer life.

Older reel mowers, and there are still some of them around, were heavy in weight and hard to use. Modern technology has allowed the use of durable, light alloys which are much preferable. Advertising claims, notwithstanding, English reel mowers are unlikely to be any superior to those manufactured elsewhere, although they are likely to be far more expensive.

Rotary Mowers

Whether powered by electric motor or, more frequently, by gas engine, the rotary mower is the most familiar mower to Canadian and American gardeners. A deck covers the blades, which operate on a horizontal plane. The machine comes with four wheels at the sides (all adjustable in height), a motor or engine on top, and handles with which to steer.

Many rotary mowers sold today come with an automatic mulching attachment to shred the cut blades of grass finely, before depositing them back onto the lawn. This returns nutrients and does not, despite garden-fence folklore, cause any increase in thatch. This attachment is an excellent innovation, and allows you to avoid having to use a bag to catch the mowings, or a mighty compost heap to absorb them all.

Unfortunately, although rotary mowers are used widely, they do not equal adequate mowing. Far from it in fact. The blades of rotary mowers are seldom sharpened even by professional operators. Hence, they tend to tear rather than cut cleanly (as a reel mower does). You can prove this yourself by plucking a blade of grass from the lawn immediately after mowing. Hold it up and examine the cut edge closely. It will likely be ragged, ripped, and torn at by blunt blades.

This also bruises the ends of the grass, so that twenty-four hours after cutting the entire lawn takes on a faint brown sheen.

When purchasing electric, or gas-powered rotary mowers, it pays to examine various features other than the price.

Mowing Width

Wider is not better – it may make the mowing more cumbersome and slower if there are many narrow, hard-to-access areas to be mown. A width of forty-five centimetres (eighteen inches) is satisfactory for most suburban gardens, sixty centimetres (twenty-four inches) will work on large properties with uncomplicated lawn shapes and no steps to lift the mower up and down.

Self-Propelled

This is not necessarily better than a hand-pushed model, particularly where there are intricate areas to be mown. A self-propelled machine will normally only be purchased for those lawns that are not quite large enough to warrant a ride-on model; and, as with anything which increases the number of working parts, the greater its risk of breakdown.

Height Adjustment

This is absolutely essential as grass is not always mown at the same height throughout the season. Most machines are adjusted by raising or lowering the wheels, but many and varied are the ways this is achieved. Check in the store to see how easily and smoothly the height adjustment method works and never, ever fall for the sales pitch "it may be stiff now, but it will become easy later."

Grass Catcher

Side-mounted grass catchers may predominate the market, but they make mowing in confined spaces or along flower or herb borders difficult; rear-mounted grass catchers are entirely more satisfactory. Make sure they attach securely, and that they disconnect smoothly and easily. Remember, if you have purchased a machine with a self-mulching attachment, you may not need a grass catcher at all.

Servicing

Sharpening the blade and cleaning the air filter are two essential and frequent servicing chores. If access is not easy, and fittings poorly designed, look elsewhere.

Tools

Wheelbarrows were invented in SW China in the first century B.C. by a semi-legendary personage, Ko Yu. The first mention of this fact is by Kan Pao in 348 A.D. The oldest surviving picture is from a Han Dynasty Hsuchow Tomb first seen in the West c.1122 in a stained glass window from Chartres Cathedral.

Spare Parts

> *I should like to protest against the statement that I have ever called a spade a spade. The man who did so should be condemned to use one.*
>
> Oscar Wilde

Sooner or later even the best designed machine is going to require some repair: wheels break, control cables snap, spark plugs need replacing. Does your sales outlet carry these parts in good supply – forget the line "we can order it in." Canadian Tire stores have a well-deserved reputation for excellence and their "Mastercraft" house brand offers excellent value.

Ride-on Mowers & Tractors

In the 1940s and 1950s, gardeners who mowed lawns were referred to as "grasshoppers." Times change: now professional lawn maintenance workers are known deprecatingly as "lawn jockeys." Perhaps they can find comfort, and a new career, in a new sport, the Motor Mowing Grand Prix, which the British humourist, Michael Bentine, claims to have invented. Bentine, it should be noted, was at one time associated with the *Goon Show*.

Large sweeping lawns which would make eighteenth-century English landscaper, 'Capability' Brown, green with envy, are manicured today with ride-on mowers or tractor-mounted mowers. Sheep were used to do the job in Brown's day. One might be justified in wondering if the fleecing has ever ceased when pricing some of today's lawn equipment.

Tractors are expensive to buy, and they are not cheap to maintain. However, I recommend purchasing a tractor rather than a ride-on mower because the latter has but a single purpose: cutting the grass. Garden tractors, like their big brothers, are available with various attachments. In addition to the rotary mower, there will likely be a trailer, plus a cultivator at the very least. Most rural dwellers will find the snow plough attachment of even more interest.

Purchase such tractors from authorized dealers only, dealers who also have the facilities and staff to service what they sell. Inquire around to determine where local professional lawn and garden maintenance contractors purchase tractors, and other similar powered equipment. Remember, down time for them equals major financial losses, which they are unwilling to tolerate.

Although we examine the safety aspects of all equipment and tools later in this text, we cannot overemphasize that operating a garden tractor can be extremely dangerous. While trying to mow up a slope, just a quarter turn of the rear wheels backwards can tumble the machine over, trapping the hapless operator underneath. The number of agricultural workers who have died in this manner is enormous, and the numbers of homeowners injured greater still. Statistics in the U.S. show that three thousand people came to grief with garden tractors within a single year.

Garden Tractors
Purchasing Points
- always try before your buy
- options include rotary and reel mowers, sweepers, disc edgers, snow blowers and blades, chippers and shredders, power blowers amongst others
- bagging the cuttings is sometimes essential and should not be an "option"
- decks of mowers vary in size but a larger or wider deck does not necessarily get the work done faster
- dealers supplying property maintenance contractors are usually very reliable
- demonstration of all equipment, on site if possible, is essential
- diesel engines, preferred by many experienced operators, are available on some compact tractors
- differential lock allows the rear wheels to pull together, useful when the going gets rough
- dumping trailers are a useful accessory
- financing is extremely competitive amongst dealers and manufacturers – it pays to check carefully
- manoeuvrability is essential, especially in tight spaces and around trees
- mowers may be front, under, or rear-mounted
- mulching blades are essential and should not be an "option"
- power steering is available on some compact tractors
- repairs under warranty should result in a "loaner," available if the repair will last anything over a few hours
- serviceability ease at home is essential
- side discharge is preferable to keep cuttings out of borders and beds
- spare parts must be immediately available, not flown from Foochow, Fukien in China
- snow removal can require considerable power
- tool mounting may be the classic 3-point hitch on rear, or other – always check how easy and quickly this can be done
- consider a contour following, wheel-mounted, rotary mower for uneven lawns
- make sure warranties are for both tractor and power train with equipment

Hand Tools and Equipment

Rakes

Gravel rakes have stiff tines set at approximately ninety degrees to the handle. They are invaluable in removing modest thatch build-ups, less so when carelessly thrown down with the tines pointing up. Treading on them, tines up, may result in un-garden-like language.

Leaf rakes, also known as fan- or spring-tine rakes are, not surprisingly, used for raking leaves from the lawn. They are efficient, quiet, do not pollute, are long-wearing, and neighbourhood friendly. Use them also to remove lawn clippings, when these are not desired to be left on the lawn.

Shears

A simple, short-handle pair of garden shears may be used for edging lawns, to trim formal hedges, prune coniferous evergreens, and slice back perennials in late fall. In order to use shears properly, one must kneel, as Kipling observed:

> *Adam was a gardener, and God who made him sees*
> *that half a proper gardener's life is spent upon his knees*

This is fine when one is young. The older one gets, however, the more favour one finds in using a long-handled pair of shears, even if they cannot be used for much else.

Turf Edger

Use this instrument every few weeks to put a fresh edge on your lawn wherever it meets borders, beds, paths, and driveways. This implement has a curved, half-moon blade on a long handle. It is also used to cut the sod neatly when laying a new lawn. Keep sharp with a flat file.

Trowel

A narrow-bladed or bulb trowel is an excellent weapon to remove larger weeds. Choose those with a business end of stainless steel, and a wooden handle. The latter absorbs shock better while being comfortable in cooler weather, and does not slip when wet.

Rake Superstition

In Britain it is believed that if a gravel rake is left with the prongs pointing upwards it will shortly rain, and, of course, in England it so often does.

Knife

The use of kitchen carving knives to remove weeds from the lawn is to be discouraged. It causes marital strife and terrifies the neighbours. A grafting knife is an ideal choice. Available from superior garden centres, some bulb and seed mail-order firms, and specialty tool suppliers. It has a sturdy, hooked blade with a thick and heavy back.

Fertilizer Spreader

Many garden centres loan lawn fertilizer spreaders with purchase of the fertilizer. These are usually of the "Cyclone" form, as granules of fertilizer fall down through an aperture at the base of the hopper when a knob is operated on the handle. The fertilizer hits a spinning plate (activated by the wheel movement) and is thrown out with some force to the sides and in front of the spreader. A baffle prevents discharge to the rear, so the operator avoids coating. If kept in good repair and properly adjusted the "Cyclone" spreader gives fast and reasonably accurate coverage. It may, however, be difficult to avoid unintentional overlapping coverage of lawn strips. This can cause irregularities and, in the worse scenario, your lawn gains the appearance of a yellow and green zebra. When spreading weed-and-feed type fertilizers, be very careful that nearby flower beds and borders are not treated as well.

Another alternative is the drop spreader, wherein the fertilizer granules move down and through calibrated holes at the bottom of the hopper, this time by a perforated bar at its base. The bar is activated by movement of the wheels. No fertilizer is thrown out to the front and sides. The drop spreader is very accurate when used properly in its application, but takes longer than its "Cyclone" cousin to cover the same area. Many keen gardeners prefer drop spreaders.

Small urban plots or awkward areas in larger lawns may be serviced by small hand-held spreaders. Miniature "Cylcone" types have the plate at their base which is set spinning by movement of a hand crank on one side. And, yes, that is the right side for left-handers. These spreaders are also excellent vehicles for overseeding small to medium size areas of grass.

Sprayers

You must consider carefully whether investing in anything more than a cheap watering-can for applying herbicides is a wise move. If you are using the chemical route to bring weeds under control, and you follow that with proper culture, it should not be

> ## Spade Beliefs
>
> *If you wave a spade at some one, it will bring them bad luck unless they throw soil at you. Never bring a spade into the house over your shoulder or a member of the family will die.*

necessary to use chemicals again. If you do require more chemicals, or need them on larger properties, it might be wiser, more economical, and certainly safer to contract out to a specialized lawn care company. The simple truth is that residues of hormone selective herbicides are incredibly difficult to remove from equipment. Unfortunately, your garden's most desirable ornamentals, herbs, vegetables, and fruit are all equally sensitive to the slightest traces of these chemicals.

Liquid "weed-and-feeds" may be obtained from local garden centres. These fertilizers come packaged in their own hose-end applicator. Already blended with the nozzle adjusted correctly, they make an excellent compromise for suburban and smaller rural lawns. Use the ubiquitous green plastic watering-cans sold everywhere to treat urban lawns. Make sure these come with their own sprinkler head – known to older traditional gardeners by the confusing denomination of "rose." A coarse sprinkler of this type means there is far less danger of accidental wind drift onto surrounding ornamentals or edibles. Use an indelible pen to write "Danger – Herbicide" on the side of the can. If your neighbours' dogs are damaging your front lawn, add a skull and crossbones. Place the watering can prominently on the lawn. Fill it with water to prevent it blowing away. Even though dogs cannot read, this display will have an amazing effect.

Aerators

Power aerators (which are almost invariably gas-engined) are expensive pieces of equipment in which to invest, even when used twice a year as recommended. Rent from stores specializing in such services. You may also wish to consider suggesting to your neighbours that they might like to share benefits and costs. The average suburban lawn can be aerated in an hour or less. If your neighbours also use the equipment, their lawns will be improved as well, lessening the spread of obnoxious pathogens and weeds.

Filament Trimmer/Edgers

Originally designed to keep weeds down along farm fences lines, these devices from hell take second place only to leaf-blowers in their decibel disturbance. Used without sufficient precaution, they are also dangerous. Stones, pieces of glass, wood chips and other debris may be hurled with injurious force when coming accidentally into contact with the filament. Professional garden and park maintenance personnel wear hard hats equipped with a clear plastic face shield, heavy gloves, long pants and safety boots, along with ear protectors when operating power trimmers.

Even then, they leave a curbed edge rather than a vertical one where the lawn meets flower beds and borders. Why do ground crews use these tools? They are fast, require minimal skill, and make enough noise to prove that the operators are antisocial – a trait regarded as desirable in the trade. The name of one trimmer currently on the market tells it all: *"Wild Thing."*

Power Equipment

Owners of large properties or those who are neither young nor fit will find power equipment essential. All but the largest gardens, or those of vacation homes not serviced with hydro, would be better off using electrically-operated equipment. Operators who complain that the cable interferes with their work should be aware that self-charging battery models of almost everything are now available. Electric motors are quieter and do not pollute the air. And because they do not require filling with gas or oil, there is no risk of spilling some on the lawn.

Dethatchers

These are not required as often as aerators, so there is even less reason to purchase rather than rent. As with aerators, though, when renting, see who else in the immediate neighbourhood might wish to use one at the same time.

Leaf Blowers

Many irate city and suburban dwellers consider these machines banshees that should be banished. "Not so," reply garden maintenance contractors. Leaf blowers

are essential equipment we cannot do without. Homeowners have shown a reluctance to invest in these devices so far. Electric-powered models are offered but many claim these to be inefficient. Alternatively, there are vacuum attachments available for filament trimmer/edgers, complete with a bag. Unless you have a large, heavily treed garden, it is probably economically and environmentally sound to stay away from the back-pack mounted professional leaf blowers. Los Angeles (where more Canadians live than in most cities in Canada) has recently banned them. Toronto, Canada's largest city, keeps blowing hot and cold over the idea.

Power Edgers

Power edgers are available in both electric motor and gas engine powered forms. The electric model features shears or, better still, a wheel-mounted circular blade under a protective shield. This acts rather like a skil saw and is equally efficient. Power edgers leave behind a beautiful, vertical, clean-cut edge to the lawn, one that is equal to that of a turf edging tool or shears.

Maintenance and Storage

The old adage claims a poor workman always blames his tools. A modern version might be that one can always recognize a poor gardener by the way s/he maintains and stores tools. The mania for use and dispose implements is ebbing fast, but I suppose many of us still have a rusting pile of carelessly cast away tools and machinery in a dark recess at the back of the garage. And of course an operator's manual *did* come with the lawn mower . . . but where is it?

Hand Tool Tips

- Clean off clinging soil, dirt, and other debris after each use; old toothbrushes are excellent for this purpose.
- Wipe down all metal parts with a lightly oiled rag
- Hang on a proper tool rack, or from hooks mounted in a garage or other dry, protected place
- Use a flat file regularly to put a sharp edge on turf edgers, as well as spades and hoes
- Sharpen shears and garden knives with a carborundum or "whet" stone
- At the end of each season, sand wooden handles smooth and cover with a coat of urethane or rub down, in the old-fashioned but effective way, with warm linseed oil.

Tips for Equipment
- Clean off clippings and other debris after each use, especially under mower decks
- Wipe all metal parts with a lightly oiled rag
- Check the engine's air filter at least monthly and clean as necessary
- Fuel two-stroke engines with exactly the gas/oil mixture recommended in the owner's manual
- Rotary mower blades will require sharpening monthly: disconnect the spark plug or electric power cable; spread newspaper and turn over on to this surface; remove blade and sharpen with a flat file; replace balance by the centre of a pencil, making sure it is absolutely level (if not, use the file to remove slightly more metal on the side that is too heavy); remount securely
- At the end of the season, have reel mower blades professionally sharpened
- Gas-powered mowers should have their fuel tanks and lines emptied at the end of the season as fuel will deteriorate if left sitting over winter. Remove the spark plug, pour a tablespoon of lubricating oil into the cylinder and, with the spark plug still out, turn over the motor once to coat the inside of the cylinder; replace the spark plug loosely and store in a dry, safe place for the winter. Don't forget both the loose spark plug and its disconnected cable when attempting to restart the following spring.

Safety

Gardeners are a notoriously hardy and long-lived species. Modern machinery carelessly used can cut off any budding gardener with sudden and startling thoroughness. Sixty-three thousand people tangle with lawn mowers and leaf blowers, snow ploughs, and throwers in the United States each and every year. Here are some tips to make sure you maintain your place in the long-lived gardener's group:
- Wear suitable clothing: loose, flapping shirts may be comfortable in hot weather, but they can easily be caught and pulled into power equipment
- Wear protection: filament trimmers/edgers and leaf blowers at the very least call for ear protectors, work gloves and boots, plus some form of eye shield (more than eyeglasses)
- Walk the lawn prior to every mowing and remove debris such as stones, glass, bark chips, or anything that might be thrown by the mower blades, causing injury and damage to the machine
- Do not mow while barefoot or wearing flimsy shoes: a foot slipping under the deck of a rotary mower can result in a fast toe amputation
- Change and launder all clothing after applying any pesticide (insecticide, fungicide, herbicide, etc.) even those regarded as "natural"
- Never allow children or irresponsible persons to use power equipment of any sort
- Never carry passengers, especially children, aboard ride-on mowers or tractors

- Never operate equipment or use tools while inebriated
- Allow gas engines to cool before refueling and, to avoid damage to the lawn, do so only on a driveway or other paved area
- Do not smoke while refueling gas-powered equipment
- Disconnect the spark plug cable before servicing any gas-powered equipment
- Remove the power cable plug from the socket before servicing any electric-powered equipment
- Replace frayed electric power cables immediately after the damage is noted
- Never operate electric equipment under wet conditions

Ground Covers

*While no doubt pleasing to a cow, a lawn can hardly engage the intellect of
human beings.*
                                                                    Tung Chu-in (1936)

L
awns have their limits. In some areas they are either unsuitable or require
an inordinate amount of attention. Other forms of ground cover are needed in such places.

Steep slopes of more than thirty degrees planted with grass not
only become extremely hard to cut, but extremely dangerous as well. One
slip while pushing a hand mower, one wrong move while sitting on a tractor or
ride-on, can result in tragedy. Today, it is not purely because of environmental concerns that municipal park departments allow such inclines to return to more natural conditions, or replace grass with what the horticultural industry is pleased to call
"alternate ground covers."

Grass of any species will not thrive in dense shade, where it is undesirable to
thin the trees or prune branches up to a height of three metres (ten feet) from the
ground. Nor will grass grow well under trees with very shallow root systems
(Silver Maples and Weeping Willows, for example) since the trees compete with
grass for moisture and nutrients.

Hillside properties divided into terraces may be appealing to mountain goats
but not to the gardener forced to lift a mower up and down the different levels. The
work is tiring, hard on the back and, if sufficient care is not exercised, dangerous.

Vacation homes are not optimum sites for lawns either. Several hours each and
every summer weekend spent behind a roaring, belching mower or atop one, cultivating several hectares of grass is not normally regarded as anything close to R & R
(rest and relaxation). Enormous lawns on very large properties will also consume
time better spent relaxing elsewhere, or sampling the delights of other horticultural products suitably fermented.

Ground covers combine with shrubbery and trees to reduce total lawn area
without sacrificing an attractive open appearance. They are not an answer for anyone seeking a garden that maintains itself. Ground covers must be watered, fertilized and cultivated just as other parts of the garden are – albeit on a less demand-

ing schedule. Ground covers must also be weeded during the years they take to become established.

Ground covers are not cheap. Perennials such as bugleweed *(Ajuga* spp.*)* may appear less expensive at first than deciduous or evergreen shrubs, but large numbers of the former are required to cover the same area as the latter. A square metre (about one square yard) covered by one shrub may require as many as nine or ten perennials planted at thirty centimetre (one foot) centres. Good quality ground covers can cost $20 a square metre, even when purchased in large quantities at discount prices. Sod, by comparison, runs somewhere about ten percent of this cost, or $2 a square metre, although sod may be more costly to maintain later.

Any area selected for ground cover installation requires the same amount of preparation as a new lawn requires, whether sodded or seeded. You will need to spread at least fifteen centimetres (six inches) of home compost or composted animal manure (cattle, sheep or horse). Despite metrification, manure continues to be sold "by the yard," i.e. by the cubic yard. One cubic yard will cover thirty-six square feet (about four metres) to a depth of six inches (fifteen centimetres), not exactly a large area. Put another way, a large dump truck holds some twenty cubic yards (some fifteen cubic metres), which will cover seven hundred and twenty square feet (seventy square metres) to a depth of six inches (fifteen centimetres). This is approximately the size of an average suburban Canadian front yard.

Next you will need to add at least a kilogram of bone meal, a natural, slow-releasing fertilizer, for every one hundred square metres (one thousand square feet) of compost, and dig the whole lot under. That's right – dig, using what a politician would call a soil-inversion implement, but what gardeners know as a spade. A square-nosed spade is the most efficient, but on soil heavily invaded by roots from surrounding trees and shrubs, one with a round or pointed nose will be easier. Sharpening the spade's business end with a flat file prior to commencing operations will make your work even easier.

And your existing lawn, weed-ridden as it is? What does a farmer do after he has let a field "lie fallow" for a year or more? He ploughs everything under, knowing that weeds, properly inverted to fifteen centimetres (six inches) or more, cannot make it up again. Better still, weeds add more organic matter to improve the soil.

Why not make things easy and use a rototiller? Have you seen a farmer turning a field under with one of these pathetic excuses? Tillers were invented to prepare seed beds after ploughing. Used continuously, they will destroy the tilth of the soil and cause drainage problems by creating a "pan" or impervious layer at the maximum depth of their tines (and that maximum depth is hardly something to boast about). Good, farm tractor mounted tillers may reach down eight or nine inches. The heaviest rear-mounted tine, self-propelled models may possibly reach eighteen though more like ten centimetres (four to six inches). Front-tine tillers are about as efficient as a kitchen blender, scratching away at the sod like a demented chicken. A spade reaches down thirty centimetres (twelve inches) or more, and inverts the soil properly, without destroying its structure – or destroying the peace and tranquillity of the neighbourhood.

Prepare your new lawn area by removing all stones, roots, and other debris, then rake roughly. If no natural slope exists, shape one which will promote a slight drop away from the house to permit safe drainage. Allow your soil bed to stand for a week after preparation so it can be worked by sun, wind, hungry birds, and predacious insects. The birds and insects will clear away most of the grubs, their larvae, eggs, and weed seeds. On the morning of planting, rake the bed lightly once again, and let it set for a few hours to allow the sun and wind to shrivel up any weed seedlings that have had the audacity to germinate. If your intention is to plant needle-bearing or broad-leaf evergreens, spread seven centimetres, or three inches, of Canadian sphagnum peatmoss over the bed to slightly lower the pH of the soil.

Once you have collected your plants from the nursery, or have had them delivered, keep each one well-watered and in a shaded area until ready to plant. Even if you plan to plant almost immediately, the ground cover will benefit both by being watered and by being left for an hour – unless of course, it is already in a condition in which only a frog would feel at home. Most plant stock today is supplied in plastic grow pots of whose recycling potential most garden centres are well aware of as long as the containers are returned. Pluck each plant from its pot, and position it at a depth level equal to that at which it was growing in its pot. Soil around

---

Buffalo Grass and the *Wall Street Journal*

Perhaps it was the mention of golf that attracted the powers that publish the well-known business newspaper. After all, golf courses spend an estimated $4 billion a year on maintaining their fairways and greens. Anything that can reduce that cost significantly would be worth investing in. Enter the native buffalo grass, which positively flourishes under the hot, dry summer conditions found on the Great Plains and into the Canadian Prairies.

Of course, it needed a little boosting of the genes even if described as "the hottest thing on the market." Rumours had become firmly rooted in some Canadian minds although not apparently with greens keepers. The "improvements" made allow the new, improved buffalo grass to grow from south of the Mason-Dixon line in a wide band across the midwest to northern California and southern Oregon. Not included are the Great Lakes area, any of the upper United States – or Canada

Perhaps someday somewhat altered crabgrass – and other native species, let it be noted – will emerge from the laboratories of Calgary University as a truly Canadian solution. Of course when it does, the government will tax it out of existence and the inventors will return to experimenting with canola.

shrubs and larger perennials must be firmed down with several stamps of a boot heel; more delicate and smaller specimens are firmed down with fingers or the handle-end of a planting trowel. Apply a generous helping of liquid transplanter fertilizer to complete the job. Plant Products of Brampton, Ontario, manufactures an extremely superior form of fertilizer for this purpose, as does Wilson (who adds rooting hormones to their product for extra effect).

Some evergreen ground covers are still sold with their roots wrapped in sacking, a condition known to horticulturists as "balled and burlapped." Never, ever attempt to remove this covering before planting. Instead, place each plant, burlap and all, in its hole. Then half-fill the hole with soil and tamp the soil down. Every last piece of sacking and any accompanying cord or twine should be untied or cut away from the base of the shrub and folded back into the hole. Never remove these items. Fill the hole completely up and leave the wrapper to rot away as the roots grow through it. Almost every evidence of nursery wrapping will disappear in a year or so.

One of the reasons most ground covers fail to "take" is not the lack of proper and/or thorough soil preparation, but the lack of sufficient watering follow-through after planting. Most soils require one centimetre (one-half inch) of water every three days, but leaving the sprinkler running for an hour at average municipal water pressure does the job nicely.

Do you need to mulch the newly-planted ground cover? A bark chip mulch in spring or early summer is not only attractive but will help reduce moisture loss and prevent weeds. In those parts of the country without assured winter snow – which insulates and protects the perennial's crown – a different sort of mulch is recommended: thoroughly composted two-year-old leaf material is magnificent. Straw, spread late in fall in the afternoon and watered down so that it does not blow around, is another option. Never, ever use hay, which any farmer's son or daughter can tell you is substantially different from straw. Hay is full of a variety of

Andorra Juniper

weed seeds, waiting until the following spring to sprout and infest the ground cover. Winter mulches should be applied well after the first heavy frost and removed only as the perennials emerge the following spring.

Do selective herbicides keep weeds under control? Newly-planted or young perennials and woody plants can be overly susceptible to chemicals their older relations will tolerate. On the other hand, it may take several seasons of pesticide build-up before one discovers that a particular brand of selective herbicide is lethal. This may be a cautionary role for commercial growers. The home gardener has today's most efficient and environmentally-friendly weed control devices available close at hand. These are known as fingers.

Ground Covers - Selections

Andorra Juniper (Juniperus horizontalis plumosa)

Andorra junipers grow thirty centimetres (one foot) high and spread two to three metres (six to eight feet) at maturity; the foliage turns a plum colour in winter. As with all junipers, the Andorra must have full sun and, once established, tolerates drought admirably. A compact form is sometimes offered but is of little use as a ground cover except in very restricted areas.

Bearberry or Kinnikinick (Arctostaphylos uva-ursi)

Kinnikinick is native to Canada, and grows in sandy, acid soils, which may be a hint as to why, although frequently recommended, it does less well in our heavier populated and/or gardened areas, which lack such conditions. Bearberry is very attractive where it will thrive, and should be planted at one to one-and-a-half metre (three to five-foot) centres in full sun. It has pinkish blooms in spring followed by red berries which last all winter. The berries have given it its common name, as bears emerging from hibernation apparently eat them to relieve constipation. Our Aboriginal peoples smoked the leaves of this low evergreen shrub as a tobacco substitute.

Bugleflower or Bugleweed (Ajuga reptans)

Several selections of this vigorous perennnial exist, although the variegated forms are harder to find than others. A low prostrate with the ability to spread almost everywhere, this plant should be kept well away from lawn edges and from rockeries where, unfortunately, it takes root all too often. This ground cover has attractive blue flowers in spring and is best planted alongside paved paths and driveways at thirty-centimetre (twelve-inch) centres.

Bergenia or Giant Rockfoil (Bergenia cordifolia)

Bergenia was a great Gertrude Jekyll favourite. She used it to soften the edges of natural stone paths. It is also attractive when planted under magnolia trees or native serviceberry. Its enormous leathery leaves resemble those of waterliles: waxy green above, maroon below (seen when the wind happens to lift them momentarily). Low and ground hugging these plants are highly effective in smothering weeds. They produce unusual spikes of pink flowers in spring. Plant at forty-five centimetre (eighteen inch) centres in full sun.

Crown Vetch *(Coronilla varia)*

Crown vetch rarely seems to succeed in Canadian gardens despite its favourable writeup in many international works on ground covers. It has been more successful when used alongside highways to control erosion of slopes, but even there it seems to have been replaced by other choices. Crown vetch will grow in the most appalling soils with little or no fertilization, but it does require full sun.

Day Lilies *(Hemerocallis species and hybrids)*

Day lilies are not often thought of as ground covers. They are an excellent choice particularly for erosion-prone slopes in sun or shade, even in face of severe tree root competition. The old fashioned tawny orange or lemon yellow forms are extremely economical, and can be planted at forty-five centimetre (eighteen inch) centres. Today's modern hybrids offer better selection in colour and scent. They are not always vigourous, however, and are likely to command considerably higher prices.

Dead Nettle *(Lumium species)*

Some of the older forms of these low-growing perennials tend to be somewhat weedy, although renewed interest in the dead nettle today has resulted in the development of some most attractive selections. These, like most perennials used as ground covers, should be planted in sun or shade at twenty-four to thirty centimetre (twelve to eighteen inch) centres.

Douglas or Waukegan Juniper *(Juniperus horizontalis douglasii)*

This juniper is still planted as a ground cover, in addition to its ornamental uses. It is utilized perhaps more so in those western states and provinces which originated so many of the excellent species now in cultivation.

Dwarf Phlox or Moss Pink *(Phlox subulata)*

These sun-loving plants produce low, mossy mats of white or bright red and pink blooms in late spring. They are an excellent choice for edging. Widely available at modest prices, moss pinks should be far more widely used as ground covers than they are. Plant thirty centimetres (one foot) apart in well-drained, sandy loam.

Dwarf Pine or Mugo Pine *(Pinus mugo)*

Mugo pines are evergreen ground covers for those areas with light shade, as

Phlox

well as full sun. They are hardy up to sub-arctic zones. Plant at two-to-three metres (six-to-eight foot) centres with generous additions of peatmoss to the soil. Fertilize very early each spring. Encourage dense bushing by pinching the "candles" or young, soft shoots about halfway down in late spring before they harden off.

English Ivy *(Hedera helix)*

English ivy is especially effective in coastal British Columbia and south-western Ontario along the shores of Lake Erie and Lake Ontario to Toronto. Its survival rates elsewhere are low. These plants are evergreen and will root anywhere and everywhere, quickly forming a dense mass in deep, moist loam. They tend to smother shrubs and small trees under such conditions, and must be kept clipped back. English ivy's aerial roots may damage brick, mortar, and woodwork when grown on the side of houses or other buildings, although it does impart an old world charm.

Goutweed *(Aegopodium podagraria)*

The only reason for including this vile plant is that it is far too prevalent in existing gardens, large and small, urban, suburban, and rural. While the species does have plain green leaves, its variegated form is commoner. Both are equally invasive. Only a masochist or politician could love goutweed, which expropriates all space available. It remains one of the few good reasons for chemical herbicides in the garden. I only wonder why garden centres keep selling the plant.

Japanese Spurge *(Pachysandra terminalis)*

Japanese spurge is too often recommended as an easy alternate to periwinkle, but it really requires a deep, rich, moist loam – free from tree root competition. These plants are effective under oaks with deep root systems, but much less so under maples. Japanese spurge is hardy over most northern terrain, but flourishes on the West Coast. Plant at thirty centimetre (one foot) centres in shade or sun.

Lily-of-the-Valley *(Convallaria majalis)*

Lily-of-the-valley was Queen Victoria's favourite flower and surely, after well over a century of use, deserves a rest. These plants tolerate shaded, poor growing conditions and will even flower under such. The blooms, with their familiar scent, appear in spring. Unfortunately the red berries which follow and all other parts of the plant can cause cardiac arrest when sampled. Nevertheless, lily-of-the-valley is a favourite target for slugs, and by summer usually takes on a somewhat battered appearance.

Ostrich Fern *(Matteuccia struthiopteris)*

Most ferns are not vigorous enough to make suitable ground covers except under the most optimum conditions. Ostrich fern will flourish in deep, moist, shaded soil, although it may take several years to become firmly established. Try to purchase these ferns in large, twenty-five centimetre (ten inch) diameter pots for more rapid filling of the area desired. Be prepared to wait at least five years before harvesting the tightly curled young shoots in spring for that gourmet delight, fiddleleaf greens.

Pachistima *(Paxistima canbyi)*

Fortunately, Pachistima is offered less and less in retail outlets. Slow growing, not hardy in cooler areas, it demands sandy, acid soils. There are far better ground cover choices available today.

Periwinkle *(Vinca minor)*

Say "ground cover" and most people immediately think "periwinkle." Even though this plant is becoming more and more overused, it thoroughly deserves its reputation. Once established, it will flourish in shade or sun with minimal care. The only major causes of plant failure are lack of proper soil preparation and planting too far apart. Much nursery stock offered today, skimpy, barely rooted and in cell-packs, is a disgrace to the horticultural business. Try to find well-grown eighteen centimetre (six inch) diameter pots and plant at thirty centimetre (one foot) centres in rich, well-prepared moist loam. Let the plants grow untouched for a year. Late in the next year's spring, set your mower blades at three inches from the ground and mow the entire area to encourage spreading rather than upright growth.

Hosta

Plantain Lily *(Hosta species and hybrids)*

Of especial use amongst taller shrubs or under small trees, these perennials from the north-east Orient are too familiar to require any description. Flourishing in moist shade or equally moist sun, they vary enormously in appearance. In general, smaller-leafed forms should be chosen for smaller gardens and larger forms for more generous areas. Plant hostas at thirty to sixty centimetre (twelve to twenty-four inch) centres anytime the soil can be worked. Although there are frequent complaints of slug and snail damage, particularly in moister areas, this is largely cosmetic.

Moreover, there are now some modern hosta hybrids on the market which claim to be "slug resistant," although how they fare when faced with the infamous West Coast "banana slug" has not been stated.

Reptan Juniper *(Juniperus virginiana reptans)*

This is another native Canadian juniper which has found favour as a ground cover planted at six-foot centres in full sun. Junipers in the wild frequently clamber over rocky slopes, so garden situations with similar terrain, including rockeries, are ideal.

Ribbon Grass, Gardener's Garters or Canary Grass *(Phalaris arundinacea picta)*

"Gardener's garters" was the delightful English traditional name of this ground cover, before political correctness took umbrage and opted for the more prosaic "ribbon grass." This is one of the few true grasses which makes a reliable and vigorous ground cover. It will grow in light shade or full sun. Plant at thirty centimetre (twelve inch) centres in good, well-drained loam and (as with all grasses) wait until early spring before cutting back the previous season's dead growth.

Ribbon Grass

Roman Chamomile *(Chamaemelum nobile)*

Herb enthusiasts swear by this ground cover as a substitute for grass. Others who have tried swear at it! Roman chamomile needs full sun, a well-drained good loam and some shearing. It will thrive under these conditions, and will even withstand being walked on or, according to one herbalist, sat upon, following the example of medieval lords and ladies.

Red Thyme *(Thymus serpyllum 'Coccineus')*

Red thyme is vigorous and quick-spreading in sunny, light, and well-drained soils. Like most thymes, it withstands modest foot traffic and, as a bonus feature, releases a delightful scent. This plant is often recommended, along with the two selections mentioned below, for planting between patio slabs where it effects both weed and bug control. Plant at thirty centimetre (one foot) centres. Many garden centres, for reasons known best to themselves, attempt to substitute this more mounding form for woolly thyme. The original form, known as mother-of-thyme, has purplish flowers.

Roses *(Rosa hybrids)*

Sick and tired of flyer delivery pathogens? Stop them, and keep snowmobilers and dirt bike morons at bay by using *rosa* hybrids. Any rose candidate for ground cover use must require far less pampering and be much more hardy than domestic plants. Fortunately, Agriculture Canada has worked for several decades to produce suitable candidates from the "Explorer" and "Parkland" series. We particularly recommend 'Charles Albanel,' 'George Vancouver,' 'Henry Hudson,' 'John Davis,' 'Louis Jollieet,' 'Morden Blush,' 'Royal Edward' and 'William Booth.' Light shade to full sun is required for each, with a good soil. Plant at one to two metre (three to six-foot) centres. None of these roses requires winter protection and maintenance is minimal.

Sargent's Juniper *(Juniperus chinensis 'sargentii')*

Most junipers of Chinese origin are thoroughly at home in northern climate conditions and will flourish. This low form is as prickly as the familiar upright 'Mountbatten' (introduced from a seedling at Sheridan Nurseries in the late 1940s). Plant at two metre (six foot) centres.

Silver Mound *(Artemisia schmidtiana 'nana')*

This is a beautiful low lying member of the wormwood tribe. Its foliage may appear so soft and delicate as to invite stroking but don't let that fool you; this is one very tough perennial, one which spreads with astonishing rapidity. Plant at forty-five centimetres (eighteen inch) centres alongside paved paths and driveways in full sun.

Skogholm Cotoneaster *(Cotoneaster dammeri 'Skogholm')*

Cotoneaster is a small prostrate evergreen shrub about one metre (three feet) in diameter with masses of small white flowers in the spring followed by red berries in fall. It is a most attractive shrub and makes an excellent ground cover with year-round interest. Skogholm is more vigorous than the species, *C dammeri*, and probably a better choice than the rockspray cotoneaster, although many garden centres and landscape contractors may substitute the latter two indiscriminately.

Snow-in-Summer *(Cerastium tomentosum)*

Valuable for its silver-grey foliage and masses of white flowers in early summer, snow-in-summer has weedy habits which detract from its beauty. In fact it is closely related to the notorious chickweed. Snow-in-summer is excellent, however, for covering dry, sunny banks, and slopes with a dense growth that smothers out almost anything else. Plant at forty-five centimetre (eighteen inch) centres.

Sweet Woodruff (Galium odoratum)

Sweet woodruff is more familiar perhaps in the herb fancier's garden. Its delicate foliage and odour make a delightful contrast when planted close to a stone walkway. And while it may appear shy and retiring, this plant is surprisingly tough and well able to look after itself, once established. Plant at thirty to forty-five centimetre (twelve to eighteen inch) centres when using as a ground cover.

Snow-in-Summer

Tamarix Juniper (Juniperus sabina tamariscifolia)

Tamarix are probably the very finest of all junipers for use as a ground cover. They are prostrate plants, rapid growing, with a width extending up to two and one-half metres (eight feet). They have rich green foliage which will withstand extreme climatic conditions. Tamarix is the ideal choice of needle-bearing evergreen for sunny areas.

Wapiti Juniper (Juniperus horizontalis wapiti)

The wapiti juniper is not often found in garden centres and other outlets, but is a fine ground cover, particularly, as with all junipers, on sunny, or dry slopes

Wild Ginger (Asarum canadense)

This is our own native wild ginger. The European species, although sometimes available has smaller leaves and is less hardy. Wild ginger's large leaves make excellent ground cover under deciduous trees in deep rich loam, solidly mulched with composted leaves every fall. Plant at thirty centimetre (twelve inch) centres in spring or early summer. Pioneers noted that all parts of wild ginger smell of the familiar spice when crushed; they used its rhizome as a substitute for flavouring food and beverages.

Wintercreeper (Euonymus fortunei coloratus)

One of the best of the admittedly few broad-leaf evergreen ground covers available, wintercreeper may drop its foliage completely in areas with very cold winters. But it is still a ground cover worth growing. Small urban gardens would do better with the selection 'Kewensis,' although nurseries shy away from propagating the species for some reason. Plant in sun or shade at two metre (six foot) centres.

Woolly Thyme (Thymus lanuginosus)

Similar to red thyme, but more prostrate and ground-hugging with greyish, woolly foliage and attractive pink blooms.

Bulbs for Underplanting

Few ground covers look their best in spring, when almost everyone living in northern climes is suffering severe attack of cabin fever. Colour is what we need, and colour we can get by planting certain spring-blooming bulbs the previous fall. Unlike over-hyped tulips, these spring-bloomers will not only return year after year, they will actually multiply with little or no attention. And better still, squirrels hate them. You can achieve a random, naturalized look by taking a handful of bulbs, standing with your back to the area to be naturalized, throw each bulb over your shoulder, one by one. Plant each exactly where it has landed. You may wish to time your planting efforts to a period when the neighbours are unlikely to notice your actions.

Daffodils and Narcissus (Narcissus hybrids)

Narcissus, according to Greek mythology, fell in love with his own visage reflected in a pool of water. The gods, in their pity, turned him into the flower. Neither incident found much favour with Narcissus' girlfriend, the nymph, Echo. She would be even more dismayed today to discover over ten thousand narcissus varieties are registered with the Royal Horticultural Society. And, although as many as half of these are obsolete, experts estimate there are some five hundred narcissi available to the keen gardener. This does tend to limit any discussion on the merits of individual narcissus.

Plant these bulbs as early in fall as possible for best display the following spring. Thirteen to fifteen centimetres (five to six inches) deep, anywhere with good drainage, is about right. When purchasing narcissus, look for bulbs with multiple "noses" (as they are called in the bulb trade) or two or three bulbs held together in a cluster. Each nose will produce blooms. Another tip is to demand daffodil and narcissus bulbs from British Columbia. These are of equal quality and considerably cheaper than those grown in Holland. Daffodil and narcissus are some of the very few bulbs the canny Dutch do not have a choke hold on.

Daffodils have long trumpets, or centres to their blooms, and a single flower to each stem. The classic variety is 'King Alfred,' an all-yellow form now entering into its second century of glorifying gardens. Narcissus have short trumpets and, while some stems bear single flowers, many are multi-flowered. A few treasured varieties carry on the delicious scent of their ancestors: 'Cheerfulness,' 'Yellow Cheerfulness' and 'Suzy.' Plant these bulbs within the ground cover, close to a walkway or door used everyday in order to enjoy an aspect of the garden all too often overlooked.

Daffodils and narcissus foliage takes a long time to die back. If you remove these bulbs prior to die back, the chance of blooms forming the following season is greatly diminished. Fortunately, said foliage is a true illustration of the wonders of underplanting in ground covers. Their display bursts forth and dies back long before perennials have really acknowledged that spring has arrived and that it is time to rise from beds. By that time, though, daffodil and narcissus foliage commences to look distinctly unappealing. Luckily, they are concealed by the new growth of the later blooming ground covers.

British Columbia's Saanichton Peninsular, north of Victoria on Vancouver Island is a spectacular site for viewing these early spring blooming bulbs in all their glory. Take the bus from downtown Vancouver to Victoria in early spring, and the ferry across the Strait of Georgia. You will land about a half-hour north of Victoria. Much of the run down to the provincial capital is through fields filled with enough daffodils to make Wordsworth envious.

Scilla or Siberian Squill (Scilla sibirica)

Plant scilla eight centimetres (three inches) deep in September or October, right in the middle of your lawn. Group in patches of a dozen or so bulbs. Scilla produces delightful small blue flowers, and it is almost always one the cheapest bulbs available. Pink and white species can also frequently be found at the same low prices.

Scilla is the classic bulb which gives the blue flush to early spring lawns in older, more established parts of our cities. It is one of the earliest bulbs to flower, usually slightly before or along with crocus, and one of the first to disappear later in spring – flowers, foliage and all – leaving nothing to worry about when it comes to the first mowing.

Scilla was named by the Greeks, who found it blooming close to the seashore. They used this plant as a rat poison.

Herbal Lawns

According to one English enthusiast, herbal lawns are back in fashion. All you have to do, she claims, is to dig out any clump of sod, roots and all. Replace with soil from elsewhere in the garden, then plant nice large pots of nursery-grown wild strawberry, ground ivy, pussytoes and yarrow.

Perhaps this works well in England, but here, proper preparation and plant selection is required. Even then, most experts seem to be less than thrilled with the results. Roman chamomile will withstand being walked upon as will various ornamental thymes. All these plants, however, must have full sun. None of them, all claims to the contrary, create a really comfortable surface where upon one can sprawl happily, contemplating the rest of one's garden.

As something new and different, herbal lawns are bound to have a certain appeal, probably to the herb gardener. In thyme, as the saying goes, one grows sage. Or should it perhaps be a thyme and a place for everything?

Wild Flower Meadows

Why not just buy one of the wild flower seed mixtures sold either in garden centres or through catalogues? All you will need to do is scatter the seeds around. And a few weeks later you'll have a permanent, perfect ground cover. No need to go to all the trouble and expense described! Not so.

Just as the forces of lawn and nature are not infallible, neither are promoters of "natural" life styles.

And what are "wild flowers" anyway? Are they flowers native to Canada? If so, to what part of Canada? A quick check of labels reveals that most wild flower meadow mixes frequently contain several Eurasian natives or, as botanists refer to them, aliens.

Okay, maybe you really are not worried about alien species in your garden. All you want to do is scatter the seed about and watch the flowers come. Not so easy according to many of the best and oldest suppliers of wildflower meadow mixtures. These experts recommend that first you remove all existing cover with a chemical herbicide to assure the wild flower seed has no competition. Only then do you spread the seed and hope for the best.

Assuming everything goes well, the results are unlikely to enthrall. Commerical wild flower meadow seed blends were college tested in Ontario over several years. None were found to be satisfactory. The conclusion was that the only places they might be used were to fill in remote areas of golf courses or under hydro power lines.

Ornamental Grasses

Keep off the grass. Remember when you, too, were struggling for recognition.

Sign said to be on the lawn of the Hollywood house of Bing Crosby

Ornamental grasses are still struggling to find general acceptance, but they are by no means newcomers on the gardening scene. The Japanese have been culturing various forms of a *Miscathus sinensis*, or Japanese silver grass, for centuries. Towards the end of the last century, French Impressionist painters, Cezanne, Monet, Renoir, and Van Gogh came to admire natural grasses, uncut and only marginally tamed, with their fountains of slim leaves and graceful seed heads.

The uses of ornamental grasses in the landscape are enormous. There are grasses for almost every situation one is likely to encounter. Humber Nurseries, of Brampton, Ontario, for example, carries over two hundred different species.

The larger, more vigorous grasses are best suited to larger gardens, but there are forms for ground cover, the edges and borders of perennial beds, accent plantings, backgrounds, barriers, and even containers growing on deck and patio. Municipal parks are filled with luxurious masses of plantings, while florists and amateur flower arrangers alike drool over the possibilities these plants offer, fresh and dried. Japanese style landscaping is firmly established in North America and, as the passion for Chinese dossier gains momentum here, it will offer even greater opportunities for the use of these elegant specimens.

Many ornamental grasses are chosen for their colour, in addition to their gracefulness and the sound created by the wind rustling their foliage. The warm-season forms, particularly the ever-popular Japanese blood grass, are especially welcome in fall. And almost all these species remain over winter, not to be cut back like other perennials. The winter garden is, unfortunately, often a forgotten factor of northern landscapes. Ornamental grasses help remind us of the winter beauty which can be added to the home garden.

Perhaps the best news for gardeners is the fact that ornamental grasses are a tough crowd, unlikely to suffer any particular devastation from pests or

> *Wild Oats are all very well, but not when they grow as high as a jungle.*
> Vita Sackville-West (1921)

> *It whispers in the breeze and is silent in the storm.*
>
> Arab saying of the Spanish Reed

diseases, although dogs, as always, remain a hazard.

Gardeners with shade problems, a particular concern on the West Coast and in older established urban areas, need not feel left out. The old-fashioned gardener's garters, *Phalaris* (known to the politically-correct as ribbon grass) tolerates and even flourishes in light shade as does, surprisingly enough, Japanese blood grass. Hair grass, *Deschapsia*, actually does best in shade, particularly if the soil is moist.

Signs around Toronto city parks beg citizens to "Please walk on the grass." (The instigator, the late Tommy Thompson, one time Parks Commissioner for the City of Toronto, even has the same words on his gravestone.) We'd like to add a new sign: "Please plant the grass."

A Selection of Ornamental Grasses

Blue Fescue *(Festuca ovina glauca) (syn. F. cinerea)*

Blue fescue is an xerophyte growing fifteen centimetres (six inches) tall, and requires full sun. It is a low, tufted grass which is an excellent choice near the front of a perennial border or bed. It appears to be available even in the most mediocre of garden centres. Blue fescue was popular long before the current interest in ornamental grasses and deservedly so. Despite the fact that it produces bumper crops of seeds when given the chance, it is not particularly invasive and tolerates very dry areas once established.

Blue Gramma *or Mosquito Grass (Bouteloua gracilis)*

This tall, sixty centimetre (twenty-four inch), xerophyte requires full sun. It is native to the Canadian Prairies as well as the American Great Plains, and might better be called "blue gramma," as it most emphatically does not encourage that bane of outdoor summer life. The alternate name comes from the fancied resemblance of the very prolific seed to the mosquito larvae. This grass turns a beautiful purple in the fall, and looks particularly effective when mass planted, particularly in prairie gardens. It thoroughly dislikes acidic, heavy, and poorly-drained soils.

Blue Oat Grass *(Helictotrichon sempervirens)*

Blue oat grass is tall, one metre (three feet), and requires full sun. It is one of the most beautiful of the ornamental grasses, with unmistakable true blue foliage which lasts well into the winter months. Blue oat grass does not tolerate the heavy clay soils, or the summer humidity typical of southern Ontario and Quebec well. It can be worth the extra effort required to grow, even in those areas, especially if an open, breezy and well-drained site is available with a lighter soil or raised bed.

Buffalo Grass *(Buchloe dactyloides)*

Buffalo grass reaches fifteen centimetres (six inches) in height and requires full sun. This is another classic Canadian grass native to the Prairies and American Great Plains. Its low growth makes it a fine edging for perennial and other borders, especially when under-planted with early-blooming small spring bulbs. Buffalo grass must have good drainage, but dislikes very sandy soils. Although this species spreads by stolons as well as by seed, it is slow to grow and thus, while not particularly invasive, is also a poor choice for erosion control or as ground cover.

Cotton Grass *(Eriophorum latifolium)*

Cotton grass grows one metre (three feet) tall in moist areas and requires full sun. There are many selections of cotton grasses, all of which require wet conditions to flourish. This grass can be found growing naturally in marshy areas exposed to full sun. It can become invasive under the right conditions and so must be kept carefully under control. Cotton grasses all thrive in somewhat acidic soils in cooler areas.

Fountain Grass *(Pennisetum japonicum)*

Fountain grass requires full sun, and grows to one and one-quarter metres (four feet) in height. This large group of attractive grasses is principally from the Orient. The rigours that prevail during winter over much of Canada makes these grasses suitable for planting in milder areas only. They make an excellent choice, though, with their "fox-tails" especially valued in borders and flower arrangements for their contrasting effects. Fountain grass is not particularly fussy as to soil conditions, but does appreciate extra moisture.

Gold Brome Grass *(Bromus inermis* 'Skinner Golden')

This grass grows up to one metre (three feet) in height and requires full sun. It is an excellent grass for use as a ground cover because it spreads rapidly by underground stolons. It is best avoided in smaller gardens for this reason. Gold brome grass requires nothing more than a well-drained site with no shade. It does like some extra moisture until it becomes established. Watch out for "reversion," or the sudden appearance of the original green blades of the species. Pull these out immediately.

Japanese Blood Grass *(Imperata cylindrica* 'Rubra')

Japanese blood grass grows to forty-five centimetres (eighteen inches) tall, and requires full sun to semi-shade. It is an extremely popular ornamental grass in high demand for its magnificent colour; however, this colour fades when grown in shade. Japanese blood grass requires light, sandy, well-drained soils in full sun to give the best display of colour. Since it grows to a maximum of forty-five centimetres (eighteen inches) high, it is an excellent choice for smaller gardens where it

Shade-Tolerant Ornamental Grasses
(including sedges and rushes requiring less than five hours sun a day)

Big Bluestem	*Andropogon gerardii*
Little Bluestem	*Andropogon scoparius*
Bulbus Oat Grass	*Arrhenatherum elatius bulbosum* 'Varigatum'
Fall-Blooming Reed Grass	*Calamagrostis arundinaceae brachytricha*
Bowles Golden Sedge	*Carex elata* 'Bowles Golden'
Blue Sedge	*Carex glauca*
Silver Variegated Japanese Sedge	*Carex morrowii* 'Variegata'
Drooping Sedge	*Carex pendula*
Plantain-leafed Sedge	*Carex pendula*
Creeping Variegated Broad-leafed Sedge	*Carex siderosticha* 'Variegata'
Northern Sea Oats	*Chasmanthium latifolium*
Tufted Hairgrass	*Deschampsia caespitosa*
Siberian Lyme Grass	*Elymus racemosus*
Bent Awn Plume Grass	*Erianthus contortus*
Giant Fescue	*Festuca gigantea*
Golden Variegated Grass	*Hakonechloa macra* 'Aureola'
Bottlebrush Grass	*Hystrix patula*
Japanese Blood Grass	*Imperata cylindrica* 'Rubra'
Snowy Woodrush	*Luzulea nivea*
Greater Woodrush	*Luzulea sylvatica*
Golden Grass	*Milium effusum* 'Aureum'
Silver Banner Grass	*Miscanthus sacchariflorus*
Japanese Silver Grass	*Miscanthus sinensis*
Japanese Flame Grass	*Miscanthus sinesis* 'Purpurescens'
Variegated Japanese Silver Grass	*Mischanthus sinensis* 'Variegatus'
Moor Grass	*Molinia caerulea*
Gardener's Garters or Ribbon Grass	*Phalaris arundinacae* 'Picta'

invariably attracts attention, even from that peculiar twenty percent of the population who profess not to garden.

Japanese Flame Grass (*Miscanthus sinensis* 'Purpurascens')
Japanese flame grass grows to one and one-half metres (five feet) tall, and requires full sun to semi-shade. If you notice a brilliant red ornamental grass in the fall, it is likely to be this Eulalia which holds its colour well into the winter months.

The contrast thus created against snow has to be seen to be appreciated and makes it worth growing for this reason alone. Japanese flame grass's tall plumes, over one metre (three feet) high in mid-summer, will also attract attention.

Japanese Silver Grass *(Miscanthus sinensis)*

Japanese silver grass will do well in full sun to semi-shade, growing to a height of one metre (three feet). Cultivated for centuries by the Japanese, this grass may be somewhat tender for prairie gardens, but will flourish when sufficient moisture is provided, and warm summers with milder winters prevail. It is especially effective in larger gardens and much in favour by public park planners and planters.

Jobe's Tears *(Coix lacryma-jobi)*

This annual will grow to be two metres (six feet) high, and requires full sun. It will usually survive winters in the extreme south-western areas of British Columbia. Jobe's tears is an outstanding annual in every way. Its seeds provide added interest and have been used for rosaries and beads. This grass is available as seed from specialist mail-order suppliers, and more rarely as an "annual" in garden centres. Keep it near the back of your border as, under favourable conditions with hot summers, it easily reaches the two metres (six feet) height. Jobe's tears is a sub-tropical Asian native.

Pampas Grass *(Cortaderia selloana)*

This grass will grow to a height in excess of two metres (six feet) and requires full sun. Although reliably hardy only in southern Ontario (Toronto and reportedly to Barrie) and the West Coast, this tall grass with its razor-edged leaves is an excellent choice for those gardens large enough to display it properly, or for sites requiring protection from intruders. Wear long-sleeve shirts, tough pants and choose the longest of long-handled hoes when cultivating in its vicinity. A dwarf form is said to be hardier, but *Erianthus ravennae*, Northern pampas grass, is hardier still with plumes up to over three and one-half metres (ten feet). This grass requires reasonably assured supplies of moisture.

Purple Love Grass *Eragrostis spectabilis*

Purple love grass grows one metre (three feet) tall, and requires full sun. It is native to southern Ontario and Quebec, extending to points south and west to Minnesota. It is not reliably hardy on the exposed portions of the Prairies. The grass is forty-five centimetres (eighteen inches) high when not in flower. It thrives on a blazing sun in sandy but reliably moist soils. The cloud-like purple appearance of this grass makes it highly desirable for any garden which can offer it a proper environment.

Ornamental Grasses for Cold Climates
This is list of ornamental grasses which are hardy to at least Zone 3

Big Bluestem	*Andropogon geradii*
Little Bluestem	*Andropogon scoparius*
Variegated Bulbous Oat Grass	*Arrhenatherum elatius bulbosum* 'Variegatum'
Mosquito Grass	*Bouteloua gracilis*
Skinner's Golden Brome Grass	*Bromu inermis* 'Skinner's Golden'
Buffalo Grass	*Buchloe dactyloides*
Blue Fescue	*Elymus canadensis*
Canada Wild Rye	*Festuca ovina glauca*
Moor Grass	*Molinia caerulea*
Red Switch Grass	*Panicum virgatum* 'Rehbraun'
Gardener's Garters or Ribbon Grass	*Phalaris arundinacea* 'Picta'
Northern Dropseed	*Sporobolus heterolepis*

Purple Moor Grass *Molinia caerulea*

Purple moor grass grows to two metres (six feet) in height, preferring full sun to semi-shade. The various forms of moor grasses die back to ground level and the foliage does not last into winter. This is counterbalanced by the moor grasses' extremely attractive displays during the growing season. It prefers wet, boggy and distinctly acidic soil conditions. All moor grasses do best in full sun but will tolerate light shade.

Prairie Beard Grass *Schizachyrium scoparium*

Prairie beard grass prefers full sun and grows forty-five centimetres (eighteen inches) tall. It is a member of the xerophyte family. A native grass to the North

Purple Moor Grass

American continent, prairie beard grass will double its height when in flower or seed, turn orange in the fall and keep this colour well into the winter months. Although prairie beard grass is not particularly fussy about soil conditions, it dislikes poor drainage but will tolerate droughts. It has been suggested as a ground cover because of its self-seeding ability, but can become aggressive if not controlled.

Ribbon Grass, Gardener's Garters or Canary Grass
(Phalaris arundinacea 'Picta')

Ribbon grass tolerates wet areas, but is also a xerophyte, and grows to six metres (two feet) tall. It prefers full sun to semi-shade. The English refer to this species as "gardener's garters" which is a far more interesting, if less descriptive, name than the more prosaic "ribbon grass" North Americans use. Ribbon grass is one of the few ornamental grass species that will flourish in light shade, but should be kept under careful control as it is inclined to become invasive. Ribbon grass grows in graceful arches and is not particularly fussy as to soil conditions, tolerating moist conditions and withstanding occasional flooding to a few inches deep.

Siberian Lyme Grass *(Elymus racemosus)*

Siberian lyme grass grows one metre (three feet) high and requires full sun to semi-shade. It is an excellent selection as a ground cover but should be used with caution elsewhere, particularly in smaller gardens owing to its invasive habits. This grass is tolerant of almost any soil conditions so long as it has good drainage. It has a magnificent true blue colour which is valued by both professional florists and amateur flower arrangers.

Silver Banner Grass *(Miscanthus sacchariflorus)*

Growing to a height of two metres (six feet), silver banner grass requires full sun to semi-shade. Comprising some of the most desirable of all the ornamental grasses available, the *Miscanthus* species and cultivars are known to keen gardeners and devotees of ornamental grasses as 'Eulalias.' Most ornamental grasses prefer moist, rich soils and cool climates, and silver banner does best under precisely such conditions, maintaining a display even into early winter. It is not recommended for smaller gardens, because of its invasive habits.

Tufted Hairgrass
(Deschampsia caespitosa)

Tufted hairgrass grows up to one metre (three feet) tall, and requires full sun to semi-shade. It will only grow in wet areas. There are several

Tufted Hairgrass

species of these grasses: Crinkled Hairgrass, *D. flexuosa*, actually prefers acid soils and summer temperatures cooler than many of our other popular grasses. All hairgrasses tend to be prolific self-seeders. Their fine foliage makes their use as ground covers a good bet. Note that they do best in deep, rich loam and may not be the best choice for areas under trees with heavy root competition. All are valued for use in cut flower arrangements.

Variegated Japanese Silver Grass (Miscanthus sinensis 'Variegatus')

Growing two metres (six feet) tall, variegated Japanese silver grass prefers full sun to semi-shade. Like blue fescue, *Festuca ovina glauca*, silver grass has been available to discriminating gardeners for over a century, long before the current interest in grasses emerged. One of the taller of ornamental grass selections available, silver grass might best be left to equally expansive gardens or public parks. It can also be considered for more modest areas, where the variegated foliage will bring life to dull and dingy corners, because it is one of the very few grasses to flourish in medium shade.

Giant Grasses

Bamboo

Bamboo is a giant grass of which there are over a hundred species. Some species grow over one-half metre (one foot) a day.

Spanish Reed

Arundo donax from Europe, Western Asia, and North Africa is sometimes known as "Giant Grass." It may grow to five metres (sixteen feet) high, although it is not reliably hardy here. Spanish reed is one source of musical instrument "reeds" and was formerly used for fishing rods and fencing.

German Sarasparilla

A sedge from Europe, *Carex arenaria*, also known as "German Sarsaparilla," is cultivated in Europe for its aromatic rhizome. Used in veterinary medicine as well as for arresting erosion.

Esparato Grass

Stipa tenacissima is used to make fine papers.

Lemon Grass

A tropical grass from southeast Asia, *Cymbopogon citratus* yields an oil used in toiletries. This grass is also used in the traditional cuisine of many countries such as Thailand.

Cyperus

Cyperus (Egyptian papyrus is one) have been adapted for many other uses. In China a species is used to make mats. Elsewhere in tropical Asia another is used for the same purpose. Coco grass has fragrant roots that can be used to scent clothing. English galingale, another Cyperus, can be used to extract a violet-scented substance that is sometimes added to lavender products. Several Cyperus even have edible roots.

Rushes

These moisture-loving plants are closely allied to true grasses and sometimes used as ornamentals. Many are still used for traditional basket-work, chair-bottoms and mats like tatami, the Japanese floor coverings.

Lawn & Garden Ornaments

When I was at Cambridge a friend's bedmaker in the college put her back out hanging her plastic plants up to dry. It seemed to me one of the proofs of the existence of God.　　　　Douglas Chambers, University of Toronto professor and keen gardener (1996)

The Greeks purposely located their temples in magnificent scenery. Statues and other carvings decorated these structures as well as their cities. The Romans viewed the Greeks as a source of culture and learning. Leading Roman citizens were as likely to speak Greek as they did Latin. Shakespeare, notwithstanding, Caesar's last words, a fierce obscenity, were in Greek. Caesar and his fellow Romans not only traded Greek insults, but also traded statues, both the real McCoy and excellent imitations. Marketing of Greek statuary from Italy continued down to the early years of the twentieth century; buyers and sellers did not always bother about authenticating the statue, only the price. Most of these pieces, with the exception of those destined to adorn the vast villas of nobility, were intended for display in local domestic landscape projects. Ancient Roman gardens closely resembled modern urban townhouse and courtyard gardens. Statues and other decorative items formed an essential embellishment of both. Ancient statues did not have the hard, cold, pristine whiteness we know today. Both Greeks and Romans painted their statues in vivid colours, and traces of these pigments still survive on some works, along with coloured stone inlays for the eyes. A few female statues even have provision for changing the hair style as fashions altered.

Romans also created their own statues, and no Roman garden was complete without a statue celebrating the fertility god, Priapus, placed immediately outside the door leading into the garden. Priapus statues are unlikely to find favour today, as the fertility god was represented by a rather large phallus.

The Italian Renaissance saw many advances in the arts and sciences as well as the beginning of interest in physical proofs of former civilizations. Although the excavations at Pompeii (buried by the eruption of Vesuvius in 79 AD) did not begin until 1748, there was a plethora of statuary elsewhere in Italy which had escaped the lime kilns and the condemnation of clergy from earlier, more savage times. These artworks were removed, cleaned and used to decorate the newly created landscape gardens, where they formed a direct link with the Roman past – leapfrogging conveniently over Christian shrines of the medieval era. Today many devout immigrants continue the tradition by adding plastic effigies of various saints or Jesus, or even Santa, to their gardens, along with concrete lions. Oddly enough, there are very few statues depicting Saint Fiacre, patron saint of gardeners.

The Globe and Mail featured a piece on lawn ornaments in an article happily titled a "Misgnomer": an English nobleman cast the first decorative gnomes in concrete during the middle years of the nineteenth century. That artistic aristocrat believed gnomes were real people and he located them in his rockery (another new innovation at the heights of popularity as a result of royal patronage). By the end of the 1800s, lawn ornaments were available from local stores around the world.

> ### Pink Flamingos Raise Money
> *An Albany, Georgia group used pink plastic flamingos to raise money for a park. By fall 1997, they had made $40,000 by placing the birds on home owners' front lawns and charging $25US to remove them. The suffering homeowner was allowed the privilege of deciding who the next victim would be. $2,000 a week was earned in this way until somebody made off with ten of them, worth $100 to replace.*

Canada's Prime Minister Mackenzie King spruced up the landscape at his Kingsmere estate with a half-dozen cast-iron rabbits purchased in 1933 from a Mr. Bedard, owner of a hardware store in Ottawa. King also had a large ceramic donkey led by a small boy. This sculpture was so extremely life-like in natural colours, it often fooled first-time visitors. Children adored it. In 1984, the Canadian government commissioned a study to determine the social value of lawn ornaments: total cost – $13,500.

The first flamingos were cast in concrete and produced in the United States. Some time later, an unnamed craftsman experimented with plywood cut-outs and, in 1957, advanced technology and materials permitted the first pink plastic flamingo to arrive on the scene. By 1999, plastic flamingos were outselling most other lawn ornaments . . . in addition to being associated with the nadir of taste. Disciples from the Church of the Ornamental Lawn Decorations in Pasadena, California march in their annual DooDah Parade wearing

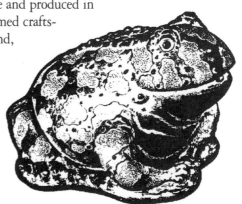

> *A stone hewn into a graceful ornamental vase or urn, has value which it did not possess, a yew hedge clipped, is only defaced. The one is a production of art, the other a distortion of nature.*
>
> Sir Walter Scott

pink flamingo hats. Proud parents of the newly-born can rent a large stork, suitably embellished with the recent arrival's vital statistics, for front lawn display.

The English remain unique in their unbridled passion for lawn and garden ornamentation. One recent British Prime Minister's father went bankrupt from making too many lawn ornaments. William Robinson, British nurseryman and prolific writer, whose career spanned the nineteenth and twentieth centuries, regarded all statuary as repose destroyers. Robinson also had scathing criticism for those gardens designed by builders with flower beds cut into geometrical shapes.

According to the London (England) Daily Telegraph, Germany is the world's leading manufacturer of garden gnomes, exporting more than a million of them each and every year. One survey of German people found that sixty percent agreed that no Teutonic garden was complete without such a figure. Presumably, they felt all gnomes need homes.

Canada, too, is a leading exporter of garden ornaments. Artists like New Brunswick's Henry Smith have found their creations (the famous leaping salmon to name one example) in such high demand that piracy of design is a major problem. One firm in Smith's home province was even hauled into court and convicted following an investigation by an undercover officer from the Royal Canadian Mounted Police (RCMP). That RCMP Division has become affectionately known as the Lawn Rangers. Another favourite design rendered in wood originated apparently from the state of Maine. We are all familiar with the elderly lady in a skirt,

seen from the rear, tending over her garden.

Not everyone believes in the social value of lawn ornaments. The mayor of one of North America's largest cities is reportedly concerned lest little people depicted playing musical instruments become known as metro-gnomes. The Society to Make Cobourg Less Tacky has taken a more aggressive attitude. This quietly beautiful lakeside Ontario town suffered a series of kidnappings. The victims were pink flamingos, plastic gnomes, and assorted other still-life, including a horse cast in concrete valued at $175.00. The society announced it was on a crusade to rid the town of tasteless ornaments. Cobourg police called it theft.

Similar tactics have been adopted elsewhere in

the world. Australia is notorious for such incidents. A fishing gnome disappeared from a lawn in Sydney. The owners began receiving postcards, apparently written by their gnome, from Queensland, where it claimed the fishing, like the weather, was much better. One fine morning a few weeks later, the owners awoke to find their gnome back home beside his pool, sporting a pair of sunglasses and a brown tan. Pink plastic flamingos disappear from lawns in the northern United States during late fall. Postcards from numerous southern cities announce that these birds have migrated, and are thoroughly enjoying the balmy winter until, come spring, they appear one by one, once again on the lawns of their presumably relieved owners.

> ## Hermits
>
> *Eighteenth-century Britain had a craze for hermitages as part of the landscape. Since real hermits were difficult to find and then get to stay, there were wax, clockwork, and even stuffed copies available.*

In spring of 1998, the Victoria, British Columbia owner of a dog-shaped lawn statue found it missing. Letters arrived in the mail enclosing photographs of the dog posing in front of various famous European landmarks. A few weeks later the dog was back at home undamaged except for a slight chip – with no explanation. Both the dog and owner appeared on national television, snapshots and all.

Lawn ornaments today span a wide and colourful range. Recent offerings include both reclining and seated pigs in pottery or pink plastic; green frogs reclining and clad in yellow polka-dot bikinis; mother ducks and their ducklings; squirrels mounted running up or running down tree trunks; raccoons, skunks, and other familiar urban animals joined by assorted dragons, gargoyles, and other mythical monsters seldom previously seen outside of the Parliament Buildings in Ottawa. The politically incorrect black jockey with a lantern, so popular in earlier years, has been reportedly seen resurrected with a Caucasoid complexion. The decline in popularity of the nude Belgian burgomaster's urinating son can only be met with relief.

Resources

In a book that has pricked many bubbles and dispelled many myths it is inevitable that one final adage now be dispersed to the winds – actually, not so much the winds as the howling gales of change. Gardening is no more timeless than any other human pursuit. Lawns, ground covers, and ornamental grasses are all subject to change and one of the great attractions of gardening is that it can be anything you make it. Changes will always take place. They always have done so.

So how can you keep up-to-date? Where can you go for more information? Professionals have an enormous and very impressive annual gathering at the University of Guelph. Sod businesses in one province host a "Turf Rodeo" each summer. The Lawn Institute of America is another source, but that is in the U.S. and little use to northern mortals.

Other help, much of it for free, ranges from provincial government turf grass experts, to free booklets. One of the best is Get a Great Lawn With All the Trimmings, from Toronto Works & Emergency Services which you can order by telephone 416-397-7100 or by fax 416-0392-2974. (If you are a disciple of organic gardening, you will love this booklet.)

One of the most concise and up-to-date government publications available, The Gardener's Handbook, offers an integrated approach to pests and disease control, striking a sensitive balance between "natural" and "chemical" answers to major problems. It is published by the Ontario Ministry of Agriculture, Food and Rural Affairs, and you can order by telephone 1-888-4-OMAFRA (1-888-466-2372) toll free but have your credit card ready. The $13 charge includes shipping, handling and Ottawa's tax on knowledge, otherwise known as GST.

Then there are the grass-roots organizations, like the California Native Grass Society, P.O. Box 566, Dixon, California 95620 (tel. 916-678-6282), which supports the preservation of Californian indigenous grasses, maintains several gardens of native perennial Graminae, and publishes the quarterly journal, *Grasslands*. Membership is $35US a year. Closer to home, Stokes Seeds of St. Catharines offers a free catalogue which contains excellent, concise advice, besides a very considerable offering of seed. Stokes has been in business for over one hundred years, and they may be regarded as reliable.

There are multitudinous websites devoted to gardening and more specifically lawns. Many professional horticulturists in private business report that maintaining such sites is expensive and inefficient. Yet others say the opposite.

We've also included a partial list of sod farms because many readers will be considering sodding in preference to seed. Our list is by no means exhaustive but we have made an attempt to strike a balance between local suppliers and those supplying a wider territory.

Even if this book consisted of nothing more than lists of contacts for further information, it would be outdated the instant it was printed. Companies, associations and even government organizations come and go with the celerity of those toadstools which pop up overnight in a lawn. The listing of any contractor herein does not imply an endorsement. Similarly exclusion does not imply lack of reliability. The author would very much appreciate hearing from any organizations which may have been left out of our source listings or whose vital statistics may have been incorrectly stated.

United States

The best place to check for lawn and turf information is the Department of Agriculture or your State Farm Cooperative Extension Services.

Other important US resources include:

Alaska Native Plant Society
Box 14163
Anchorage, AK 99154
Tel: (907) 333-8212

ANVIL (Association for the Use of Native Vegetation in Landscape)
871 Shawnee Ave
Lafayette, IN 47905

Colorado Native Plant Society
PO Box 200
Fort Collins, CO 80522

Cornell University
College of Agriculture
Ithica, NY 14853

Idaho Native Plant Society
Box 9451
Boise, ID 83707

Minnesota Native Plant Society
University of Minnesota
220 Biological Science Centre
St. Paul, MN 55108

The Lawn Institute
County Line Rd.,
PO Box 108
Pleasant Hill, TN 38578-0108

Washington Native Plant Society
University of Washington
Dept. of Botany
Box 351330
Seattle, WA 98195
Tel: (206) 543-1942

Iowa State University
134 College of Design
Ames, IA 50011

North Dakota State University of Agriculture
Fargo, ND 58105

University of Michigan
Nichols Arboretum
Ann Arbor, MI 48109-1115

University of Minnesota
College of Agriculture
St. Paul, MN 55108

University of Pennsylvania
Morris Arboretum
9414 Meadowbrook Ave
Philadelphia, PA 19118

University of Wisconsin
Wisconsin Agricultural Experimental Station
140 Agricultural Hall
Madison, WI 53706

Washington State University
College of Agriculture
Pultman, WA 99164

Canadian Federal Government
Agriculture and Agri-Food Canada
Sir John Carling Building
930 Carling Avenue
Ottawa, Ontario K1A 0C5
Tel: 613-759-1000
Fax: 613-759-6726

Canadian Provincial Governments
Alberta Agriculture, Food and Rural Development
7000 - 113 St.
Edmonton, Alberta T6H 5T6
Tel: 403-427-2727
Fax: 403-427-2861

British Columbia
Ministry of Agriculture and Food
808 Douglas Street
Victoria, British Columbia V8W 2A7
Tel: 250-387-5121
Fax: 250-953-5162

Manitoba Agriculture
Norquay Building
401 York Avenue
Winnipeg, Manitoba R3C 0P8
Tel: 204-945-3433
Fax: 204-945-5024

New Brunswick
Department of Agriculture and Rural Development
P.O. Box 6000
Fredericton, New Brunswick E3B 5H1
Tel: 506-453-2666
Fax: 506-453-7978

Newfoundland
Department of Forest Resources and Agri-Foods
Provincial Agricultural Building
Brookfield Road
P.O. Box 8700
St. John's, Newfoundland A1B 4J6
Tel: 709-729-4716
Fax: 709-729-6046

Nova Scotia
Department of Agriculture and Marketing
Joseph Howe Building
#700 1690 Hollis Street,
P.O. Box 190
Halifax, Nova Scotia B3J 2M4
Tel: 902-424-6734
Fax: 902-424-3948

Ontario
Ministry of Agriculture, Food and Rural Affairs
Communication Branch
1 Stone Road West
Guelph, Ontario N1G 4Y2
1-888-466-2372 (Toll free)
Tel: 519-826-4240
Fax: 519-826-4253

Prince Edward Island
Department of Agriculture and Forestry
P.O. Box 2000
Charlottetown,
Prince Edward Island C1A 7N8
Tel: 902-368-4880
Fax: 902-368-4857

Quebec
Ministere de l'Agriculture, des Pecheries et de l'Alimentation
2000. ch Sainte-Foy
Quebec, Quebec G1R 4X6
Tel: 418-643-2673
Fax: 418-646-0829

Saskatchewan
Agriculture and Food
Walter Scott Building
3085 Albert Street
Regina, Saskatchewan S4S 0B1
Tel: 306-787-5140
Fax: 306-787-0216

Yukon
Renewable Resources
Agricultural Branch
P.O., Box 2703
White Horse, Yukon Y1A 2C6
Tel: 867-667-5838
Fax: 867-393-6222

Sod Suppliers United States

American Sod Corp
PO Box 861
Pataline, IL 60078-0861
Tel: (800) 358-4769
Fax: (847) 934-4782
email: americansod@msn.com

Ampac Seed Co
32727 Highway 99E
PO Box 318
Tangent, OR 97389
Tel: 541-928-1651
Fax: 541-928-2430

Cascade International Seed Co.,
8483 W. Slayton Rd.,
Aumsville, OR 97325
Tel: 503-749-1822
email: cascade1@grass-seed.com

Crosman's Seeds
507 West Commercial St.,
PO Box 110
East Rochester, NY 14445

Fine Lawn Research Inc.,
PO Box 666
Albany, OR 97321
Tel: 541-926-2275
Fax: 541-924-9720
email: info@finelawn.com

Huber Ranch Sod Nursery
PO Box 188
Route 41
Schneider, IL 46376
Tel: 1-800-533-0552
219-552-0552
Fax: 219-552-0752

Western Productions Inc.,
PO Box 491
Woodburn, OR 97071
Tel: 503-982-8655
Fax: 503-981-4636

Wilco Farmers
200 Industrial Way
PO Box 258
Mt. Angel, OR 97362
Tel: 1-800-382-5369

Williams Lawn Seed
PO Box 112
Maryland, MO 64468-0112
Tel: 660-582-4616

Canada

A & M Sod Supply
R.R. #1,
Delaware, Ontario N0L 1E0
Tel: 519-652-3539
Fax: 519-652-3530

Anderson Sod Farm
36422 Hyde Bunker Rd,
Mission, British Columbia
serving a wide area, call for details
1-877-826-2383

Beverly Turf Farms
R.R. #3,
Beaverton, Ontario L0K 1A0
Tel: 1-800-665-9291
705-426-7070

Blue Grass
101 21 Barlow Trail NE,
Calgary, Albeta
Tel: 403-226-0468

Bluegrass Sod Farms
245 Oakland,
Scotland, Ontario N0E 1R0
(Supply local area)
Tel: 1-800-665-9593
519-446-3631

Blue Grass Sod Producers Ltd.
Lot 53, Red River Drive,
St. Norbert, Manitoba, R3V 1L2
Tel: 204-269-3052
Fax: 204-269-1310

Blue Grass Sod Farm
Box 11, Site 2, R.R. #1,
Red Deer, Alberta T4N 5E1
Tel: 403-347-7211

Boynton Bros. Sod
12805 Hwy 27,
Nobleton, Ontario
(south of King Road)
Tel: 905-859-4469

Brayford Sod Farms
P.O. Box 831,
Alliston, Ontario L9R 1V9
705-435-7707
1-800-461-1210

Brouwer Sod Farms Ltd.
23965 Warden Ave.,
Keswick, Ontario L4P 3E9
Tel: 905-476-4361

Canadian Independent
900 19th line,
Richmond Hill, Ontario L4E 3R2
Tel: 905-883-1292

Cedar Lane Services
39 Thirteen Mile Crossing,
Bishop's Falls, Newfoundland A0H 1C0
Tel: 709-258-7272
Fax: 709-258-7272

Chinook Sod Farm
Box 1
Aldersyde, Albeta T0L 0A0
(High River)
Tel: 403-652-5659
Fax: 403-652-5639 fax

Chris Trambert & Son,
1025 2nd Line E.,
Sault Ste. Marie, Ontario P6B 4T5
Tel: 705-949-9400
Fax: 705-946-4612

Clement Turf Farms
3330 Old Vernon Rd,
Kelowna, British Columbia V1X 6P3
Tel: 250-765-9479

Compact Sod
1400 Middle Block Road,
Cambridge (Green Horizons)
Ontario N3H 4R6
Tel: 519-653-7494 Cambridge
Tel: 519-767-2422 Guelph

Eagle Lake Turf Farms
Box 2130,
Strathmore, Alberta T1P 1K1
Eric Heuver, owner
Tel: 403-235-8873
Fax: 403-934-6813

Ellison Nursery & Turf
5450 Anderson,
Kelowna, British Columbia V1X 7V4
Tel: 250-765-8674
Fax: 250-765-8604

Elm Tree Turf Farms
9507 - 378th Ave. (Island Road),
Oliver, British Columbia V0H 1T0
Tel: 250-498-3094

RESOURCES

English Lawns Ltd.
2545 Derbyshire Way,
North Vancouver,
British Columbia V7H 1P9
(supplier & installer)
Tel: 604-929-7732
Fax: 604-924-3693

Evans Turf Farm
1844 Thatcher Rd,
Nanaimo, British Columbia V9X 1T3
Tel: 250-753-2157
Fax: 1-877-753-2157

Fairlawn Sod Nursery
R.R. #5, 17100 Concession 1,
Tilbury, Ontario N0P Q1O
Tel: 1-800-265-3212
Fax: 519-682-1524

Fairwood Sod Farms
Markham, Ontario
Tel: 905-640-8613

Fisher Landscape
258 Exeter Rd,
London, Ontario N6L 1A3
Tel: 519-652-6752
Fax: 519-652-1841

Fraser Valley Turf
41310 Yale Rd.. W,
Sardis, British Columbia V2R 1A9
Tel: 1-800-416-4114
250-823-4114

Gem Sod Inc.
524 Beaver Dam Rd, NE
Calgary, Alberta T2K 4W6
Tel: 1-800-340-6756
403-273-8673
Fax: 403-273-8752

Gem Sod Inc.
R.R. # 3
Fort Saskatchewan, Alberta T8L 2N9
Tel: 1-800-340-6757
780-998-1220
Fax: 780-992-1189

Hamilton Sod
2907 Hwy 6 South,
Mount Hope, Ontario L0K 1W0
Tel: 905-389-1315

Harvey Davis
Cameron Lake,
Mt. Uniacke, Nova Scotia B0N 1Z0
Tel: 902-866-4466

**Highland Redi-Green
Turf Farm**
16897 Windsor Rd.,
Pitt Meadows,
British Columbia V3Y 1Z1
Tel: 604-465-9812
Fax: 604-465-9805

Hildebrand Sod Farm
Box 15 (Se 11-17-8E)
Stead, Manitoba R0E 1Z0
Tel: 204-635-2188

Hollandia Nursery Sod
3725 Regional Rd. 15,
Chelmsford, Ontario P0M 1L0
Tel: 705-897-5146
Fax: 705-897-5964

Island Grown Sod
56 East Royalty Rd.,
Charlottetown,
Prince Edward Island P1A 7J7
Tel: 902-628-6402
Fax: 902-628-6402
Email r.chapel@PEIsympatico.ca

La France Sod
R.R. #1
Campbellford, Ontario K0L 1L0
Tel: 613-475-2198
Fax: 613-475-2198

Lavington Turf Farms
5770 Petworth,
Vernon, British Columbia V1B 3E4
Tel: 250-549-2967
Fax: 205-545-8566

MacDonnell Turf Farms
3345A Bulman,
Kelowna, British Columbia V1X 7V1
Tel: 250-765-4240

Manderley Sod
3090 52 St. SE
Calgary, Alberta T2B 1N2
Tel: 1-800-661-8315
403-273-8558
Fax: 403-248-1526

Maritime Sod
Box 117, West Victoria St.,
Amherst, Nova Scotia B4H 3Y6
Tel: 902-667-7413

Maritime Sod
Lower Mills Stream,
Sussex, New Brunswick
Tel: 506-433-3156

McConnell's Sod Supply Ltd.
P.O. Box 67,
Wolfedale, Nova Scotia B0P 1X0
Tel: 1-800-878-6015
902-542-2791

McEwan Bros. Ltd.
899 Holmes Road,
West St. Paul, Manitoba R4A 7A7
Tel: 204-338-0351
Fax: 204-339-0172

Musquodoboit Valley
R.R. #1,
Elderbank, Newfoundland V0N 1K0
Tel: 902-384-2233

Nashville Sod Supply
Woodbridge, Ontario
Tel: 905-851-2171

New Brunswick Quality Sod
1189 RT 2 Hwy,
Maujerville, New Brunswick E3A 8K5
Tel: 506-357-2268
Fax: 506-357-3009

Niagara Sod
1703 South Service Rd.,
St. Catharines, Ontario L2R 7L8
Tel: 905-984-8448

Ontario Sod
2376 Royal Windsor Rd.,
Oakville, Ontario L6J 4Z2
Tel: 905-257-8795

Pembina Landscaping & Sod
629 Pembina Ave. E.,
Winkler, Manitoba R6W 4A5
Tel: 204-325-9943

Petersen's Turf Farms,
2381 Manotick Stn. Rd. R.R. #1
Osgoode, Ontario K0A 2W0
Tel: 613-821-2863
Fax: 613-821-4683

Ponderosa Sod Farm Ltd.
5201 North Island Rd., R.R. 225
Compartment 2,
Courtenay,
British Columbia M9N 5M9
Tel: 250-334-2344

Porcher Enterprises
276 Apache Trail SS
(Lot 22 McPhillips)
St. Andrews, Manitoba R3C 4A3
Tel: 204-334-6062

Quality Sod
Nova Scotia
902-384-3439
email: Granview@hotnail.com

Saanich Tuff-Turf
4060 Blenkinsop,
Saanich, British Columbia V8X 2C2
Tel: 250-721-5300
Fax: 250-721-5344

South Ridge Sod
(Ottawa South, Kingston, Quebec)
2408 Manotick Stn. Rd., R.R. #1
Osgoode, Ontario K0A 2W0
Tel: 1-800-267-9772
613-821-3764
Fax: 613-821-3811

Star Sod Supply
Farm is located in
Newmarket, Ontario
Tel: 905-895-7034

Sun Valley Turf Farms
Kamloops Vernon Hwy, Box A7,
Westwold, British Columbia V0E 3B0
Tel: 250-375-2474
Fax: 250-375-2476

Sydney Landscaping & Nursery
24 Maple Ave.,
Sydney River, Nova Scotia B1S 1J6
Tel: 902-564-9910
Fax: 902-564-3075

Tasbow Sod Ltd.
Wellington Dyke, R.R. #1,
Port Williams, Nova Scotia B0O 1T0
Tel: 902-542-5563
Fax: 902-542-5308

The Lawn Doctor
P.O. Box 13813,
Paradise, Newfoundland A1B 4G3
Tel: 709-782-2990
Fax: 709-834-7991

Thompson Sod
Se 10-17-8E, General Delivery,
Stead (Gull Lake)
Manitoba R0E 1Z0
Tel: 204-635-2654

Tuf Turf Sod Farm
3608 52nd St. SE
Calgary, Alberta T2B 3K4
Tel: 403-236-7354
Fax: 403-207-1221

Westcoast Instant Lawns
4295 - 72 St.,
Delta, British Columbia V4K 3N2
Tel: 604-946-0201

Weston Turf Farms
4196 Telegraph,
Cobble Hill, British Columbia V0R 1L0
Tel: 250-743-4879

Witmore's Landscaping Sod
3708 RT 2 Hwy,
Island View, New Brunswick E3E 1G3
Tel: 506-472-3357

Valley Sod Landscaping Ltd
R.R. #4,
Bridgetown, Nova Scotia B0S 1C0
Tel: 902-665-2645
Fax: 902-665-2645
email: valsod@ns.sympatico.ca

Zander Sod Co. Ltd.
Jane & Hwy 9,
Schomberg, Ontario
Tel: 416-363-8089

Ornamental Grass Sources
US

AAA Ornamentals
7 S 273 Mary Drive
Big Rock, IL
Tel: 630-556-4310
FAx: (630) 556-9978
email: mailto:info@hostas.com

American Ornamental Perennials
29977 SE Weitz Lane
Eagle Creek, OR 97022
Tel: 503-637-3095
Fax: 503-637-3096

Broadmead Nursery
3610 Broadmead Road
Amity, OR 97107
Tel: 503-943-2155
Fax: 503-843-2232
email: broadmead@macnet.com

Creekside Gardens
155 Nix Rd.,
Chehalis, WA 98532
Tel: 360-748-6158

Fairweather Gardens
PO Box 330
Greenwich, NJ 08323
Tel: 609-4451-6261

Forestfarm
990 Tetherow Rd.,
Williams, OR 97544-9599
Tel: 541-8446-7269
Fax: 541-8446-6963

Harris Seeds
60 Saginaw Dr.,
PO Box 22960
Rochester, NY 14692-2962
Tel: 800-514-4441

New England Bamboo Company
Box 358
Rockport. MA 01966
Fax: 508-546-1075

Pride Corners
122 Waterman Road
Lebanon, CT 06249
Tel: 1-800-437-5168
860-642-7535
Fax: 860-642-4155
email: pcfservice@gyral.com

Rock Spray Nursery
PO Box 693
Truro, MA 02666-6769
Tel: 508-349-6769
Fax: 508-3449-2732
email: kherrick@rockspray.com

Tradewinds Bamboo Nursery
28446 Hunter Creek Loop
Gold Beach, OR 97444
Tel: 541-247-0835
email: Bambugib@harborside.com

Willow Pond Nursery
PO Box 192
Hewlett, NY 11557
Tel: 516-374-2522
Fax: 516-374-0533

Canada

Aimers Seeds
a modest selection is listed under
Graminae in the $4.00 catalogue
81 Temperance St.
Aurora, Ontario
L4G 2R1
Tel: 905-461-0011
Fax: 905-727-7333

Brickman's Botanical Gardens
excellent selection available through the mail order catalogue ($3.00 refundable on first order); magnificent private botanical gardens
R.R. #1 Sebringville, Ontario
N0K 1X0
Tel: 519-393-6223
Fax: 519-393-5239

Humber Nurseries
the largest individual nursery in Canada; has over 200 ornamental grasses available; $8.00 catalogue
R.R. #8 Brampton, Ontario
L6T 3YZ
Tel: 905-794-0555
Fax: 905-794-13111

Rainforest Gardens
general perennials; selection of ornamental grasses; over 1000 items in spring catalogue ($4.00); maintains a demonstration garden
13139 - 224th St.
Maple Ridge, British Columbia
V4R 2P6
Tel: 604-467-4218
Fax: 604-467-3181

Stokes Seeds Ltd.
a modest selection of annual forms is listed under Ornamental Grasses in their free catalogue and others in the Perennial Flower seed section
Box 10
St. Catharines, Ontario L2R 6R6
Tel: 905-633-4300
Fax: 1-888-834-3334 (toll free)
Email: Stokes@stokeseeds.comm

Valleybrook Gardens
wholesale grower of grasses and herbs; specializing in perennials; publish John Valleau's Perennial Garden Guide with an excellent section on ornamental grasses
P.O. Box 8000 - 454
Abbotsford, British Columbia
V2S 6H1
Tel: 604-855-1177

Garden Ornaments

Patricia Easton
agent for Derek's Green lawn ornaments. Will provide list of retail suppliers
Jordash
PO Box 599
55 Wellan Ave.
Nobleton, Ontario L0G 1N0
Tel: 905-859-0394
Fax: 905-859-0958

Web Sites

AAA Ornamentals
www.hosta.com
American Ornamental Perennials
www.gramineae.com
American Sod Co
www.americansod.com
Ampac Seed Co.
www.ampacseed.com
Broadmead Nursery
www.broadmead.com
CanGarden
www.icangarden.com
Creakside Gardens
www.wormlady.com

Crosman's Seeds
www.crosmanseed.com
Gardengate
www.garden-gate.prairienet.org
Gardeners of the Golden Horseshoe
www.interlog.com/~ggh/ggh.htm
Gardenimport
www.gardenimport.com
Garden Net
trine.com/GardenNet/
Garden Net Guide to Internet Resources
gardennet.com
Huber Ranch Sod Nursery
www.hubersod.com
International Association of Aboriculture
www.ag.uiuc.edu/~isa
Lawn and Landscape
www.lawnandlanscape.com
Lee Valley Tools
www.leevalley.com
National Gardening Association
www..garden.org
Professional Lawn Association of America
www.placaa.org
Richters
www.richters.com
The Lawn Institute
www.lawninstitute.com
Virtual Library Gardening
www.gardenweb.com/vl/
Week-end Gardener
www.chestnut-sw.com/ webpicks.htm
Western Productions Inc.
www.tcfarm.com
Williams Lawn Seed
www.WLS.com
Willow Pond Nursery
www.willowpondnursery.com

Books

Abraham, Doc and Katy Abraham. *Green Thumb Wisdom.* Vermont: Storey, 1996

Anonymous. *Walk-Behind Lawn Mower Service Manual.* Intertech Publishing Corp., 4th edition, 1991

Andrew, Brian. *Northern Gardens.* Edmonton: Lone Pine, 1987

Brown, Lauren. *Grasses: An Identification Guide.* Boston: Houghton Mifflin, 1979

Buckley, A.R. *Canadian Garden Perennials.* British Columbia: Hancock House, 1977

Crockett, James Underwood. *Lawns and Groundcovers.* New York: Time-Life Books, 1973

Cullen, Mark. *Lawns and Landscaping.* Toronto: Sommerville Press, 1985

Fell, Derek. *The Impressionist Garden.* New York: Carol Southern Books, 1994

Greenlee, John. *The Encyclopedia of Ornamental Grasses.* Pennsylvania: Rodale, 1997

Hill, Lewis and Nacy Hill, *Lawns, Grasses and Groundcovers.* Pennsylvania: Rodale, 1995

Holme, Bryan. *The Enchanted Garden.* New York: Oxford University Press, 1982

Leveque, George and Marie-Francoise Valery. *The French Garden Style.* New York: Crescent Books, 1995

Peterson, Roger Tory and Margaret McKenny. *A Field Guide to Wildflowers.* Boston: Houghton Mifflin, 1968

Schultz, Warren. *The Chemical-Free Lawn.* Pennsylvania: Rodale, 1989

Valleau, John. *Perennial Gardening Guide, 2nd edition.* Abbotsford, B.C.:Valleybrook Gardens Inc., 1995

Woodson, R. Dodge. *Watering Systems for Lawn and Garden.* Vermont: Storey, 1996

Government Publications
Federal Government:

Buckley, A.R. *Tress and Shrubs of the Dominon Arboretum.* Ottawa:Agriculture Canada, 1980

Sherk, Lawrence C. and Arthur R. Bucvkley. *Ornamental Shrubs for Canada.* Ottawa: Canada Department of Agriculture, 1968

Province of Ontario:

Ministry of Agriculture, Food and Rural Affairs. *The Gardener's Handbook: an integrated approach to insect and disease control* Toronto; 1998

Ministry of Agriculture, Food and Rural Affairs. *Weed Control in Lawns & Gardens,* publication 529. Toronto; 1998

City of Toronto:

Works and Emergency Services. *Alternative Groundcovers.* (seasonal information sheet) Toronto, June 1997

Works and Emergency Services. Gardening - *Make the Mulch of It!.* (seasonal information sheet) Toronto, June 1997

Works and Emergency Services. *Get a Great Lawn With All the Trimmins.* Toronto, 1998

Works and Emergency Services. *Grass Seeding Tips.* (seasonal information sheet) Toronto, June 1997

Works and Emergency Services. *Let Your Neighbours Know Your Lawn Is Chemical-Free.* (information sheet) Toronto, N.D.

Works and Emergency Services. *Natural Receipes for a Pest-Free Garden.* (information sheet) Toronto, April 1996

Works and Emergency Services. *Organic Lawn Care.* (seasonal information sheet) Toronto, May 1997

Works and Emergency Services. *Organic Insecticides and Fungicides for the Garden.* (information sheet) Toronto, April 1996

Works and Emergency Services. *Xeriscaping.* (seasonal information shee) Toronto, June 1997

Periodicals

Horticulture Review (Monthly). Horticultural Pulbishing Division, Landscape Ontario, Station Main, Milton, Ont. L9T2X8 (expecially valuable for the OMAF bulletings from Guelph

Landscape Trades (9 times a year). Horticultural Pulbishing Division, Landscape Ontario, Station Main, Milton, Ont. L9T2X8

Lawn and Landscape Magazine informative US turf magazine